Jesus Silences His Critics

Jesus Silences His Critics

by
John MacArthur, Jr.

WORD OF GRACE COMMUNICATIONS
P.O. Box 4000
Panorama City, CA 91412

All Scripture quotations, unless noted otherwise, are from the *New Scofield Reference Bible*, King James Version. Copyright © 1967 by Oxford University Press, Inc. Reprinted by permission.

Library of Congress Cataloging in Publication Data

MacArthur, John F.
  Jesus silences his critics.

  (John MacArthur's Bible studies)
  Includes index.
  1. Jesus Christ—Conflicts. 2. Bible. N.T.
Gospels—Criticism, interpretation, etc. I. Title.
II. Series: MacArthur, John F. Bible studies.
BT303.M25 1987   226'.206   87-1577
ISBN 0-8024-5313-9

1 2 3 4 5 6 7 Printing/LC/Year 92 91 90 89 88 87

Printed in the United States of America

Contents

These Bible studies are taken from messages delivered by Pastor-Teacher John MacArthur, Jr., at Grace Community Church in Panorama City, California. These messages have been combined into a 4-tape album entitled *Jesus Silences His Critics*. You may purchase this series either in an attractive vinyl cassette album or as individual cassettes. To purchase these tapes, request the album *Jesus Silences His Critics*, or ask for the tapes by their individual GC numbers. Please consult the current price list; then, send your order, making your check payable to:

WORD OF GRACE COMMUNICATIONS
P.O. Box 4000
Panorama City, CA 91412

Or call the following number:
818-982-7000

1
Our Obligation to God and Government

Outline

Introduction
A. The Battle
  1. A familiar text
  2. A familiar proverb
    a) The privilege of paying taxes
    b) The refusal to pay taxes
B. The Background
  1. The leaders' jealousy of Jesus
  2. The leaders' questioning of Jesus
    a) Jesus' parables
      (1) The parable of the two sons (Matt. 21:28-32)
      (2) The parable of the vineyard (Matt. 21:33-46)
      (3) The parable of the wedding feast (Matt. 22:1-14)
    b) The leaders' reaction

Lesson
  I. The Aim (v. 15)
 II. The Approach (v. 16)
  A. Their Fakery (v. 16*a*)
  B. Their Foes (v. 16*b*)
    1. Their origin
    2. Their occupation
  C. Their Fellowship
  D. Their Flattery (v. 16*c*)
    1. Dignity
    2. Integrity
    3. Honesty
      a) Proverbs 14:12
      b) Psalm 1:6
      c) Matthew 7:13-14

Introduction

A. The Battle

Matthew 22 describes the final week of the earthly ministry of Jesus Christ. As He moves to the cross, we will see the confrontation He had with the religious leaders of Israel.

1. A familiar text

Matthew 22:21 is a familiar verse. Jesus said, "Render, therefore, unto Caesar the things which are Caesar's; and unto God, the things that are God's." It's a text familiar not only to Christians but to non-Christians as well. It is used in different ways to justify many things. To understand that important statement, you need to study the context of the entire passage with the scenes and events that take place.

2. A familiar proverb

You may be aware of the proverb that says that only two things are inevitable: death and taxes. The United States Internal Revenue Service had a budget in excess of 2 billion dollars in 1984—and their only function is to collect taxes. Their headquarters are in Washington, D.C., and they have 7 regional offices, 59 district offices, and approximately 13,500 field agents, 4,460 office auditors, 2,800 special agents, and nearly 70,000 other employees. They have data on virtually every citizen in the United States. Taxation is of major importance in American society.

a) The privilege of paying taxes

If the American public stopped paying their taxes, government services would no longer be available. We depend on the taxation system to provide a safe and secure life. Americans should thank God for placing them in a country that experiences the kind of freedom and prosperity they enjoy. The United States government is a benevolent government, not a totalitarian government. That doesn't mean everything the government does is right, but Americans are nonetheless to be thankful. Taxation is an element of the prosperity Americans enjoy.

b) The refusal to pay taxes

In spite of those positive considerations, the American church is besieged by those who say Christians should not pay taxes. They say taxes are both unconstitutional and ungodly. Taxation has become a crucial question because of the following ruling by the IRS: on January 1, 1984, all church employees were made subject to the Social Security tax. Church employees (with the exception of pastors, who are considered to be self-employed) were levied a 6.7 percent tax on their wages. The church itself had to make up that 6.7 percent reduction or see their employees suffer the loss. Their payroll had to rise 7 percent if their employees were to break even.

Many churches refused to pay that tax. When a pastor wrote asking, "Should we pay the tax?" I wrote back and said yes. We were barraged with letters from other pastors who believed I was giving ungodly counsel. Often they reasoned that since money is given by parishioners to the church, it is given ultimately to God. We are not, then, to give it to an ungodly government. Fortunately, Matthew 22:15-22 addresses that dilemma.

B. The Background

On Monday of the last week of His earthly ministry, Jesus rode into Jerusalem on a donkey and was hailed the Messiah. On Tuesday He chased the money changers out of the Temple. He would be crucified on Friday and rise from the dead on Sunday. On Wednesday, however, the crowd was alarmed because the day after they hailed Him Messiah He had overthrown the Jewish religious system instead of the Roman government. The crowd didn't know how to fit that into their expectations of what the Messiah was supposed to do.

On Wednesday Jesus went back into the Temple He had cleansed, teaching the good news of the kingdom of God. The magnetism of His personality and the dynamics of His teaching fascinated the people.

1. The leaders' jealousy of Jesus

Jesus made the Jewish religious leaders irate. They resented Christ because He unmasked their pride and self-righteousness. They not only resented Him because He opposed their religion but also because He fascinated the people. Envy and jealousy filled their hearts. They resented His purging the Temple without their permission. He was genuine, and they were hypocrites. He threatened their system of self-righteousness, which was opposed to God's system of faith.

2. The leaders' questioning of Jesus

The leaders stopped Him while He was teaching and asked, "By what authority doest thou these things? And who gave thee this authority" (Matt. 21:23). The leaders wanted Jesus to show them His credentials. They were in effect saying, "Show us Your rabbinical ordination papers. Prove to us that You have the right to say what You are saying." Jesus then asked them a question. When they refused to answer, Jesus in turn said, "Neither tell I you by what authority I do these things" (v. 27). In three separate parables, He made clear that they were under the judgment of God.

a) Jesus' parables

(1) The parable of the two sons (Matt. 21:28-32)

Jesus said, "A certain man had two sons; and he came to the first, and said, Son, go work today in my vineyard. He answered and said, I will not; but afterward he repented, and went. And he came to the second, and said the same. And he answered and said, I go, sir; and went not. Which of the two did the will of his father? They say unto him, The first. Jesus saith unto them, Verily I say unto you that the tax collectors and

11

the harlots go into the kingdom of God before you."

Jesus was saying that the chief priests and the elders were like the second son, who said he would obey but did not. The leaders kept saying they were going to obey God but never did and as a result would be kept out of the kingdom. Tax collectors and harlots were like the other son, who defied God at first but in the end repented and obeyed.

(2) The parable of the vineyard (Matt. 21:33-46)

Jesus then said, "Hear another parable: There was a certain householder, who planted a vineyard, and hedged it round about, and dug a winepress in it, and built a tower, and leased it to tenant farmers, and went into a far country. And when the time of the fruit drew near, he sent his servants to the farmers, that they might receive the fruits of it. And the farmers took his servants, and beat one, and killed another, and stoned another. Again, he sent other servants more than the first; and they did the same unto them. But last of all he sent unto them his son, saying, They will reverence my son. But when the farmers saw the son, they said among themselves, This is the heir; come, let us kill him, and let us seize on his inheritance. And they caught him, and cast him out of the vineyard, and slew him" (vv. 33-39).

The man who owned the vineyard (God) leased it out to the tenant farmers (the religious leaders), and they worked the land and produced the crop. When the owner sent back his servants (the prophets) to collect what was due him, they killed them. When he had no servants left, he sent his son (Christ, the Messiah), but they killed him too. Because of their wickedness, the kingdom would be taken from them and given to those who were worthy to hear the message.

(3) The parable of the wedding feast (Matt. 22:1-14)

Jesus told another parable, saying, "The kingdom of heaven is like a certain king, who made a marriage for his son, and sent forth his servants to call them that were bidden to the wedding; and they would not come. Again, he sent forth other servants, saying, Tell them who are bidden, Behold, I have prepared my dinner; my oxen and my fatlings are killed, and all things are ready; come unto the marriage. But they made light of it, and went their ways, one to his farm, another to his merchandise; and the remnant took his servants, and treated them shamefully, and slew them. But when the king heard of it, he was angry; and he sent forth his armies, and destroyed those murderers, and burned up their city. Then saith he to his servants, The wedding is ready, but they who were bidden were not worthy. Go, therefore, into the highways, and as many as ye shall find, bid to the marriage" (vv. 2-9).

Here Jesus likens the religious leaders to people who were already invited to come to the wedding feast (salvation) but would not come because they refused to honor the king's son. The king invited others to come to the feast and take their place. Jesus was again saying that the religious leaders would be kept out of the kingdom of God, and others would come in to take their place.

b) The leaders' reaction

The Jewish religious leaders felt obliged to react to His condemnation, which was a public confrontation in the middle of the Temple courtyard. Many people heard what Jesus said. Jesus devastated them with three parabolic judgments. They knew exactly to whom He was speaking (21:45). The day before, Jesus cleaned the Temple of the money changers, and now He devastated their spirituality.

13

He attacked their unbelief and rejection of Him by calling down the judgment of God against them.

In their rage to eliminate Jesus, they devised a strategy against Him. They decided to discredit Jesus by making it appear He was inciting a riot to overthrow Rome. They planned to report Him to the Romans, who were quick to squelch any rebellion that threatened their rule. Jesus would be executed for causing a riot, and their plan would be complete. The three parables of Matthew 21-22 are now followed by three questions that the religious leaders asked Jesus in the hopes of making Him appear an insurrectionist. The first of those questions appears in verses 15-22.

Lesson

I. THE AIM (v. 15)

"Then went the Pharisees, and took counsel how they might entangle him in his talk."

The word translated "counsel" refers to mutual consolation. The leaders went to the corner of the Temple and decided to trap Him in His words. It is tragic that the religious leaders of Jesus' time would not respond to His message of salvation. Instead of accepting the message of judgment, all they wanted to do was kill the One who brought them the warning. That is like a drowning man trying to kill the person who's saving him. However, they were so consumed with killing Jesus that they missed the reality of what He told them.

II. THE APPROACH (v. 16)

"And they sent out unto him their disciples with the Herodians, saying, Master, we know that thou art true, and teachest the way of God in truth, neither carest thou for any man; for thou regardest not the person of men."

A. Their Fakery (v. 16a)

"And they sent out unto him their disciples."

Why did the Pharisees send their disciples to Jesus instead of going themselves? Because they were already shown to be phonies, and it would have been foolish to go up to Jesus now and pretend to believe in Him. Instead they sent a group that Jesus did not know. They briefed their disciples thoroughly and sent them to masquerade as sincere questioners.

B. Their Foes (v. 16b)

"They sent out unto him their disciples with the Herodians."

The Herodians were pro-Rome. They supported the Romans because they had allowed Herod Antipas to continue to rule even after they occupied that area. The Herodians knew their only hope of getting another Herod in power was by Roman appointment. The different Herods themselves seemed to have courted Rome as well.

1. Their origin

The Herods were a dynasty of Edomites who ruled Palestine. There were several different Herods, including Herod the Great (Luke 1:5; Matt. 2:1-16), Herod Antipas (Matt. 14:1-12; Acts 4:27), and Herod Archelaus (Matt. 2:22).

Before Herod the Great died, he split his rule of Palestine into two areas. One son took the region of the north—the areas of Galilee and Peraea—and another took the region of the south, which encompassed Samaria and Judea. In A.D. 6, however, Herod Archelaus was deposed from the southern region. The Romans put a new governor in his place. Herod Antipas continued to rule in the north. He was the ruler responsible for beheading John the Baptist.

2. Their occupation

The different rulers in the Herodian dynasty were of Idumean—not Jewish—descent. They were secular instead of religious rulers. The Romans left them to rule in the north because it helped serve their own purposes. In the south, however, the Romans wanted full control, so they appointed a Roman governor.

The Herodians (followers of the Herods) were Jews or Idumeans who preferred a descendant of Herod ruling in the south rather than a Roman governor.

The Pharisees were vocally anti-Rome. They thought the Romans invaded their land with their paganism. The Pharisees were offended because they thought their land was ruled only by God. And when the Roman government intervened, they saw the Romans as defying God's rule. Thus they despised Roman oppression.

Many of the Pharisees belonged to a group that later became known as the Zealots. The Zealots were terrorists who started fires and caused fights in order to incite insurrections against Roman tyranny. It may be that Simon the Zealot, one of the disciples of the Lord, belonged to this nationalistic, terrorist group (Luke 6:15). If the Pharisees succeeded in trapping Jesus into making a statement about taxation, they knew they could count on this group to cause an insurrection they could easily pin on Jesus.

C. Their Fellowship

Since the Pharisees were anti-Roman and the Herodians were pro-Roman, why did the Pharisees recruit the Herodians? Because they needed pro-Roman witnesses to testify that Jesus was an insurrectionist. If the Pharisees alone accused Jesus, the Romans would be suspicious of their motives, because the two groups were enemies. They needed the Herodians on their side in order to accomplish their goal—the execution of Jesus Christ.

Why were the Herodians cooperating with the Pharisees? Because they hated Jesus also. Herod Antipas beheaded John the Baptist because John confronted him and his wife about their wicked life. And since Jesus spoke truth as John the Baptist did, they would not have wanted Jesus around either. If you closely study the latter part of Jesus' ministry, you will notice He judiciously avoided the territory of Herod's rule because of the hostility toward Him (Mark 6:53; 7:24, 31; 8:27). The Pharisees and Herodians were both against Jesus even though they didn't agree on religion or politics.

D. Their Flattery (v. 16c)

"Master, we know that thou art true, and teachest the way of God in truth, neither carest thou for any man; for thou regardest not the person of men."

1. Dignity

"Master."

The Pharisees' disciples and the Herodians were being sarcastically respectful in addressing Jesus. The Greek translated "Master" (*didaskalos*) means "Teacher." That title was the highest honor you could pay a man. It was a term of great dignity. The Talmud says that the one who teaches the law shall gain a seat in the academy on high. One who was called Master was revered above all others because he was a teacher of the law.

2. Integrity

"We know that thou art true, and teachest . . . in truth."

These men were trying to flatter Jesus by saying He was truthful (Gk., *alethōs*) and full of integrity. They were implying, "If you believe something, you will say it." The term implied honor and respect.

3. Honesty

"Thou . . . teachest the way of God."

Not only were they saying He Himself was truthful, but they also acknowledged that He spoke a truthful message. What would they have understood "the way of God" to be?

a) Proverbs 14:12—Solomon said, "There is a way which seemeth right unto a man, but the end thereof are the ways of death."

b) Psalm 1:6—The psalmist said, "The Lord knoweth the way of the righteous; but the way of the ungodly shall perish."

c) Matthew 7:13-14—Jesus Himself said, "Enter in at the narrow gate; for wide is the gate, and broad is the way, that leadeth to destruction, and many there be who go in that way; because narrow is the gate, and hard is the way, which leadeth unto life, and few there be that find it."

4. Conviction

"Neither carest thou for anyone."

They did not mean that Jesus was indifferent to people who had needs. They meant He was not swayed by other opinions. They were saying in effect, "It doesn't matter to You what anyone else believes. You are a person of great conviction."

5. Impartiality

"Thou regardest not the person of men."

Everything the Pharisees and the Herodians said of Jesus was true, but they didn't mean what they said. Their goal was to bait Jesus into causing a riot and as a result bring about His death. They were trying to flatter Jesus into making a rash statement, thereby condemning Himself.

Flattery is condemned many times in the Old Testament (Pss. 5:8-9; 12:2-3; Prov. 7:21-23; 29:5). It tends to bait someone and then set him up for a fall. Some people allow flattery to build their egos so high that they spend the rest of their lives trying to live up to them. The Pharisees and the Herodians attempted to catch Jesus by building up His ego and then forcing Him into a corner by making Him answer a difficult question.

III. THE ATTACK (v. 17)

"Tell us, therefore, what thinkest thou? Is it lawful to give tribute unto Caesar, or not?"

Their question was simple yet broached a delicate issue. Mark adds in his gospel, "Shall we give, or shall we give not?" (12:15).

A. The Key

The Greek word translated "tribute" (*kēnsos*) is the key in understanding the Pharisees' question. It was borrowed from the Latin word *census*. The Romans counted all the citizens and made each of them pay a poll tax. The Syriac Pasheda, an extrabiblical piece of literature, calls this tax "head money."

B. The Taxes

The Romans imposed many taxes on the Jews to provide services. They built aqueducts and streets. One of their great remaining architectural masterpieces in the Caesarean area is an aqueduct. They offered the benefits of military protection through the *pax Romana* or "Roman peace." Since they provided such services, they needed to receive financial compensation.

1. Property taxes

The Romans required one-tenth of the grain and one-fifth of the wine and oil from the people. The tax could be paid in its original substance or transferred into money.

2. Business taxes

As goods were transported back and forth from city to city, taxes were exacted at harbors, city gates, and major thoroughfares. That's probably what Matthew was employed in doing (Matt. 9:9).

3. Income taxes

All wage earners had to pay a 1-percent income tax.

4. Census taxes

Each individual annually paid a denarius, which was equivalent to one day's wage. This is the tax referred to in Matthew 22:17.

C. The Rebellion

This kind of taxation did not sit well with the Jewish people. They felt it was an abuse because they saw themselves as answering to God alone. They thought of themselves as under a theocracy, ruled by God. When pagan Rome imposed exorbitant taxes, they feared their money was going to Rome and not to God.

1. The specifics

In A.D. 6 a rebellion began when King Archelaus was deposed and a Roman governor was put in his place. The rebellion was led by Judas of Galilee. He gathered a group bent on insurrection. Their theme was "God is our only Lord and ruler—we will pay no taxes to Rome!" The census tax was what ignited Judas and his followers.

In Acts 5:37 Rabbi Gamaliel tells what happened to Judas: "After this man rose up Judas of Galilee in the days of the registration, and drew away many people after him; he also perished, and all, even as many as obeyed him, were dispersed." Judas died, but he fostered a cause that remained.

First-century Jewish historian Josephus, writing about the revolution of Judas of Galilee (*Wars* II. viii.1), recorded it was the Jewish attitude toward taxes that started the revolution of A.D. 66, which ended with the destruction of Jerusalem in A.D. 70.

2. The setup

If Jesus said the Jews should pay the tax, the Jews would have been angry with Him. He would have been considered anti-Jewish. However, the Pharisees didn't believe He would instruct them to do that. They believed He spoke for God, and in spite of their dislike for Him they thought He would answer the question honestly and discredit Himself in the process.

They were sure the only thing He could say to them was not to pay the tax to Caesar. They assumed He would say it was an offense to God to pay any money to a pagan government. But if He said that, He would be considered an insurrectionist. The Herodians would then report Him to the Romans. A riot would be inevitable, and He would lose His life. The Pharisees were asking Jesus an important question. There were many Zealots in the crowd who eagerly wanted a revolution.

IV. THE ACCUSATION (v. 18)

"But Jesus perceived their wickedness, and said, Why test me, ye hypocrites?"

A. Christ's Discernment (v. 18*a*)

"Jesus perceived their wickedness."

The word translated "perceived" means "to know by discernment." Jesus knew their hearts because He knows all things. You can't fool Christ. You cannot sneak up on His blind side, because He doesn't have one. He is omniscient. John 2:24-25 says, "Jesus did not commit himself unto them [the crowds], because he knew all men, and needed not that any should testify of man; for he knew what was in man." Jesus knew the question before the

Pharisees' disciples asked it, and He also knew their evil intention.

B. Christ's Directness (v. 18*b*)

"Why test me?"

Jesus wasn't intimidated by anyone. He was truthful with them and called them exactly what they were: fakers, pretenders, and hypocrites. Although He had never seen those men before, He knew they were trying to trap Him in His words. Jesus knew their hearts because He is the all-knowing God. Their flattering tongues were tipped with deadly poison as they offered the Lord a hypocritical kiss.

C. Christ's Denouncement (v. 18*c*)

"Ye hypocrites."

Hypocrisy is such an ugly sin that it is condemned severely in the Old Testament. It was also condemned within the Jewish community.

1. Rabbi Eleazar

   The Talmud quotes Rabbi Eleazar as saying, "Any community in which is flattery will finally go into exile. It is written [Job 15:34], 'For the community of flatterers is [barren]' " (*Sotah* 42*a*).

2. Rabbi Jeremiah ben Abba

   Rabbi Jeremiah ben Abba, according to the Talmud, said that four types of people do not deserve to receive the Shekinah: scorners, liars, tale-bearers, and hypocrites (*Sanhedrin* 103*a*).

Jesus' accusation of the Pharisees was serious. He again turned the tables and proceeded to unmask the plot against Him.

V. THE ANALOGY (vv. 19-21a)

"Show me the tribute money. And they brought unto him a denarius. And he saith unto them, Whose is this image and superscription? They say unto him, Caesar's."

A. The Illustration (v. 19)

"Show me the tribute money. And they brought unto him a denarius."

1. The coins

There were various coins in Palestine, including currency from the Greeks, Romans, and Hebrews. The Roman Senate could mint copper, but only the emperor had the authority to mint silver and gold. Any silver coin would have reflected the image of the Caesar who was in power. It was the common practice among kings to hail their sovereign rule. Today the practice is much the same but usually only after the ruler has died.

2. The conflict

The denarius was an offense to the Jewish person for two reasons: it was a reminder of Roman oppression, and it was seen as a violation of the Old Testament injunction against graven images (Ex. 20:4-5). If you were to visit Israel today, you would find places where you cannot take photographs because the Jews there resist the making of images. The legalistic Pharisees were offended because to them the coinage of Rome represented a blasphemous intrusion into their worship of God.

You can well imagine the Pharisees' disciples hurrying to give Jesus a coin. They assumed He was playing right into their hands. He took in His hand the silver coin with the emperor's image on it and posed a question.

B. The Issue (vv. 20-21a)

"He saith unto them, whose is this image and superscription? They say unto him, Caesar's."

That's a seemingly harmless question, but a powerful answer accompanied it.

1. The government then

Emperor Tiberius was reigning at the time of Christ. The denarius would have had the image of Tiberius's face on one side and his throne on the other. The inscription on the coin identified him as the high priest. The coinage then was not only political but religious in significance. The emperors not only believed they were high priests but also thought they were gods. Christians were killed during the Roman persecution of the church because they failed to worship the emperor. Every time a Jewish person paid a denarius with the image of Tiberius on it, he was faced with an idol, or an image.

The appearance of a comet in 17 B.C. helped prompt Augustus Caesar to inaugurate a spectacular celebration. The Roman College of Priests was assembled, and Augustus was appointed chief priest. The priests voted to absolve the sins of all the people in the Empire. Coins were made hailing Augustus as the son of a god. The Roman state then was offering salvation in addition to prosperity. The Jews were offended to give their money to the Roman government, because to them that was like paying homage to a false religious system.

2. The government now

Many today feel the same way toward their governments. The so-called "Battling Baptists" in America are offended by the thought of paying taxes to a pagan government and wage war against paying many taxes.

The U.S. government, however, is much different from the Roman government of New Testament times. America has a defined separation of church and state. There may be some areas where it is not as clear as it once was, but it is clear that the president of the United States does not claim to be God, nor do the congressmen claim to be high priests. As Americans pay their taxes they support a strictly secular government. It is easier then to sympathize with the Jewish people of Jesus' day than with the tax protestors of our own.

VI. THE ANSWER (v. 21*b*)

"Then saith he unto them, Render, therefore, unto Caesar the things which are Caesar's; and unto God, the things that are God's."

A. Obligation to Government

"Render, therefore, unto Caesar the things which are Caesar's."

The Greek word translated "render" is *apōdidōmi*, which means "to pay back" or "to give back." It refers to a debt or an obligation that is owed someone. It is not something you have a choice about. Jesus answers the Pharisees' disciples by saying in effect, "Give Caesar's money back to Caesar. He minted it. It belongs to his economy."

When they posed the original question to Jesus (v. 17), they used a different word to describe the payment of taxes (Gk., *dounai*). They were saying, "Is it lawful to give taxes as a gift?" Their perspective was that they could do whatever they wanted to with their money. And if they didn't want to give it they didn't have to. They considered paying their taxes to Rome as a gift they could choose—or not choose—to give. In answering their question, however, Jesus said to give Caesar his money back. They weren't giving him a gift but what actually belonged to him. It was a debt that must be paid.

1. The pronouncement

In Matthew 22:21 the Lord commands that taxes be paid to the government. Taxes are a debt owed the government regardless if it is an idolatrous, blasphemous government. Jesus said to pay taxes to the Roman government even though He knew that government officials were about to execute Him. Paying taxes is not a gift or a choice; it is an obligation for the benefits received. Caesar provided for the physical, social, and economic needs of the people and was entitled to receive due compensation.

a) Romans 13:1-7—Paul said, "Let every soul be subject unto the higher powers. For there is no power but of God; the powers that be are ordained of God. Whosoever, therefore, resisteth the power, resisteth the ordinance of God; and they that resist shall receive to themselves judgment. For rulers are not a terror to good works, but to the evil. Wilt thou, then, not be afraid of the power? Do that which is good, and thou shalt have praise of the same; for he is the minister of God to thee for good. But if thou do that which is evil, be afraid; for he beareth not the sword in vain; for he is the minister of God, an avenger to execute wrath upon him that doeth evil. Wherefore, ye must needs be subject, not only for wrath but also for conscience' sake. For, for this cause pay ye tribute also; for they are God's ministers, attending continually upon this very thing. Render, therefore, to all their dues: tribute to whom tribute is due; custom to whom custom; fear to whom fear; honor to whom honor."

All governments are an institution of God, as are marriages, families, and the church. If you don't pay your taxes, you resist God and incur judgment on yourself. God ordains all governments for the preservation of society. It is a sin not to pay all your taxes. You are to submit to your government. Even though some governments are evil, they are better than no government at all, because having no government leads to anarchy. The government is designed by God for protecting the good and punishing the evil. And if you do what is right, you will fulfill the will of God. God has given the government the right to punish evildoers. Policemen, soldiers, and all those in authority stand in the place of God for the preservation of society.

Likewise, as verse 6 attests, you are also to pay your taxes. The Internal Revenue Service is one of God's ministers. Don't be selective and choose which taxes you want to pay. You need to pay them all.

b) 1 Peter 2:13-17—Peter said, "Submit yourselves to every ordinance of man for the Lord's sake, whether it be to the king, as supreme, or unto governors, as unto them that are sent by them for the punishment of evildoers, and for the praise of them that do well. For so is the will of God, that with well-doing ye may put to silence the ignorance of foolish men; as free, and not using your liberty for a cloak of maliciousness, but as the servants of God. Honor all men. Love the brotherhood. Fear God. Honor the king." God wants Christians to be models of virtue and integrity in society.

c) 1 Timothy 2:1-3—Paul said, "I exhort, therefore, that first of all, supplications, prayers, intercessions, and giving of thanks, be made for all men, for kings, and for all that are in authority, that we may lead a quiet and peaceable life in all godliness and honesty. For this is good and acceptable in the sight of God our Savior."

2. The practice

Someone might object by saying, "The money really belongs to God." However, everything in the universe belongs to God, and He has commanded that some of what He has entrusted to you should be paid to the government. Others might object by saying, "The money that is given to the church is given as an act of worship. Why should the church then give any of it to the government? Isn't that giving to Caesar what should go to God?" A person gives money to the church. The church uses some of that money to pay its pastor and staff. They in turn give some of their money in taxes to the government.

You are not giving to the government what was originally given to God. The church is giving to the government what God commanded them to give in taxes. God gives man the power to obtain wealth, and He has ordained that some of it goes to the government so that society can lead a peaceable and quiet life. You don't honor God when you refuse to pay your taxes; you are disobeying Him. And when churches are told to pay the government what it is owed, they should do it out of obedience.

B. Obedience to God

"[Render] unto God, the things that are God's."

Caesar was wrong when he asked the people to worship him. Only God deserves worship. You must pay your taxes to your governing leader but are not to render to him your worship. Jesus affirmed that you are to give the government what it can rightfully demand from you: that which is social and economic. But you are not to give government what it cannot demand: that which is spiritual and religious. A problem would arise in America if the president demanded our worship by suddenly announcing that he is God and that the congressmen are high priests. We would have to refuse, because we are to worship God alone.

1. The limits of government

The apostle Peter faced a similar problem when the Sanhedrin told him not to preach the Word of God. He said, "We ought to obey God rather than men" (Acts 5:29). The government has its limits. When the government oversteps those limits and begins making demands that are spiritual in nature, you must obey God and worship Him alone.

The Soviet church is persecuted today only because of its religious convictions. As Christians, they obey every law of their totalitarian regime, but when their government demands something in the area of religious conscience, the church does not obey because the government is making claims on what belongs only to God. If Christians are persecuted, imprisoned, or killed, it should be because of their faith in God, not because of a violation of a rightful government mandate.

2. The lesson on government

You are to give the government what rightfully belongs to it. Pay back what you owe for services rendered, and reserve your worship for God alone.

VII. THE AFTERMATH (v. 22)

"When they had heard these words, they marveled, and left him, and went their way."

The Pharisees and the Herodians looked foolish in light of the Lord's answer. They were hopelessly outclassed. His answer devastated them. The fact that the Pharisees and the Herodians left Jesus is tragic. When confronted with the truth of the Word in the person of the Lord Jesus Christ, many people turn and walk away. As you study the ways Jesus silenced His critics, be sure to turn to Him as Savior and Lord if you haven't already, and ask Him to change your life.

Focusing on the Facts

1. What does Matthew 22 describe (see p. 9)?
2. What is needed to understand the importance of the statement "Render, therefore, unto Caesar the things that are Caesar's; and unto God, the things that are God's" (see p. 9)?
3. What would happen if the American public stopped paying their taxes (p. 9)?
4. True or false: All Christians pay their taxes (p. 10).
5. What events occurred during our Lord's last week of earthly ministry (see pp. 10-11)?
6. Why did the Jewish religious leaders resent Jesus Christ (see p. 11)?
7. Describe the parable of the two sons and the point that Jesus was making (see pp. 11-12).
8. What is the point of the parable of the vineyard (see p. 12)?
9. What is the significance of the parable of the wedding feast (see p. 13)?
10. Why did the Jewish religious leaders feel obligated to respond to Jesus' condemnation of them (see p. 13)?
11. What was the aim of the Pharisees after Jesus' parables of judgment against them (see p. 14)?

12. Why did the Pharisees send their disciples to Jesus instead of going themselves (see pp. 14-15)?
13. Who were the opponents of the Pharisees, and why did the groups join forces (see p. 15)?
14. True or false: The Herodians were anti-Rome. Explain your answer (see p. 15).
15. Describe the origin and occupation of the Herodians (see pp. 15-16).
16. Describe the group known as the Zealots (see p. 16).
17. Why were the Herodians cooperating with the Pharisees (see pp. 16-17)?
18. The Pharisees and Herodians agreed that they were against Jesus even though they didn't agree on either _____ or _____ (see p. 17).
19. Describe the attributes the Jewish leaders were sarcastically attributing to Jesus (see pp. 17-18).
20. What is the key in understanding the Pharisees' questioning of Jesus (see p. 19)?
21. List four types of taxes levied within the Roman Empire, and explain each (see pp. 19-20).
22. Describe the insurrection led by Judas of Galilee and its result (see pp. 20-21).
23. How was Jesus able to perceive the malice of the Pharisees (see pp. 21-22)?
24. Describe what the inscription on Caesar's coin would have communicated to the Jewish people (see p. 23).
25. Contrast the government of the United States with the Roman government of New Testament times (see pp. 24-25).
26. True or false: You can choose whether to pay taxes to the government or not (see p. 25).
27. What is the meaning of the phrase "Render unto God, the things that are God's" (see p. 25)?
28. What are the limits of government (see p. 28)?
29. You are to give the government what _____ _____ _____ _____ (see p. 29).

Pondering the Principles

1. Jesus discerned the wickedness in the hearts of the Jewish religious leaders. They were hypocritical in their thoughts and actions toward Him. Are you hypocritical in dealing with others?

Do you ask questions and make requests with wrong motives? If so, confess your sin to God, and ask Him to change this area of your life. Study the following passages: Acts 5:1-11, James 4:1-3, and John 8:3-9.

2. As a citizen on earth and a citizen of heaven, a Christian is expected to pay his taxes. It is not an option or a choice; it is a command. Are you fulfilling your obligation to the Lord by paying all your taxes? Have you refused to give the money you owe the government because you feel it is wrong or because you simply have not wanted to do so? Reread the following verses and then make restitution of any debt you owe to your government: Romans 13:1-7, 1 Timothy 2:1-3, and 1 Peter 2:13-17.

2
The God of the Living

Outline

Introduction
A. The Resurrection in General
   1. The anticipation
   2. The affirmation
     a) Extrabiblical writings
       (1) 2 Maccabees 14:37-46
       (2) The Apocalypse of Baruch 50:2–51:10
       (3) The Talmud
     b) Biblical writings
       (1) Psalm 16:9-11
       (2) Psalm 49:15
       (3) Psalm 73:24
       (4) Hosea 6:1-2
       (5) Daniel 12:2
B. The Jewish Leaders in Particular
   1. The major sects of Judaism
     a) The Essenes
     b) The Zealots
     c) The Pharisees
     d) The Sadducees
   2. The major tenets of the Sadducees
     a) Their position
     b) Their power
     c) Their profits
     d) Their politics
     e) Their passing
     f) Their preaching

    (1) Their literal interpretation of the Scriptures
    (2) Their denial of the resurrection
       (*a*) Numbers 18:28
       (*b*) Deuteronomy 31:16
       (*c*) Deuteronomy 32:39

Lesson

I. The Approach of the Sadducees (v. 23)
  A. Their Intent (v. 23*a*)
    1. The hopelessness of the Sadducees
    2. The hostility of the Sadducees
      a) John 11:47-53
      b) Mark 14:1-2
  B. Their Indignation (v. 23*b*)
    1. The hatred in the Sadducees
      a) Acts 4:1-2
      b) Acts 5:17, 28
    2. The hardening of the Sadducees
II. The Supposed Absurdity of the Resurrection (vv. 24-28)
  A. The Levirate Law (v. 24)
    1. Deuteronomy 25:5-6
    2. Genesis 38:8-10
    3. Ruth 4:10
  B. The Leading Question (vv. 25-28)
    1. John 11:25-26
    2. John 5:28-29
III. The Answer of Scripture (vv. 29-32)
  A. The Direct Approach (v. 29*a*)
    1. Jude 13
    2. 1 Corinthians 15:35-42, 50-53
  B. The Deadly Accusation (vv. 29*b*-32*a*)
    1. The accusations in general (v. 29*b*)
    2. The accusations in specific (vv. 30-32*a*)
      a) Ignorant of the power of God (v. 30)
        (1) Marriage is only for this life
        (2) Friendships are only for this life
      b) Ignorant of the Scriptures (vv. 31-32*a*)
        (1) Exodus 3:6
        (2) Genesis 26:24
        (3) Genesis 28:13
  C. The Decisive Answer (v. 32*b*)
    1. The personal relationship
    2. The permanent covenant

IV. The Astonishment of the Crowd (v. 33)

Conclusion
A. Christ's Majestic Deity
B. Christ's Commitment to Scripture
C. Christ's Affirmation of the Resurrection

Introduction

A. The Resurrection in General

1. The anticipation

It fascinates me that mankind has such an anticipation of resurrection. Built within the heart of man is the feeling that there must be a life beyond this life. Nineteenth-century Yale professor James Dwight Dana once said he couldn't believe God would create man and then desert him at the grave. Dana captured in that statement the essence of everyone's future hope.

a) By the ancient Egyptians

If you were to read the ancient Egyptian Book of the Dead, you would find it filled with the hope of life after death. For example, a boat was sealed in the tomb of Pharaoh Cheops nearly 5,000 years ago so that he could sail through the heavens in his next life.

b) By the ancient Greeks

Resurrection was a major emphasis in the ancient Greek religion. A coin was often placed inside the mouth of a corpse so he could pay his fare across the mystic river of death into the land of immortal life.

c) By the American Indians

Many American Indians used to bury a pony and bow and arrow with their warriors so they could ride and hunt in the future happy hunting ground.

d) By the ancient Norsemen

The ancient Norseman often buried horses with their dead heroes so they could maintain their triumphant rides throughout immortality.

e) By the Greenland Eskimos

Eskimo children who die in Greenland are buried with a dog so they won't have to find their way through the cold wasteland without a guide.

f) By Benjamin Franklin

As a young boy I saw Benjamin Franklin's epitaph at Christ Church in Philadelphia. Franklin wrote this to be placed over his grave:

> The body of
> Benjamin Franklin, printer,
> (Like the cover of an old book,
> Its contents worn out,
> And stript of its lettering and gilding)
> Lies here, food for worms!
> Yet the work itself shall not be lost,
> For it will, as he believed, appear once more
> In a new
> And more beautiful edition,
> Corrected and amended
> By its Author!

2. The affirmation

Man feels the pull of the afterlife. The Jewish religion is no different. In studying the Jewish writings around the time of Christ, we see the idea of a resurrection affirmed.

a) Extrabiblical writings

(1) 2 Maccabees 14:37-46—Written around the end of the second century B.C., 2 Maccabees gives us great insight into Jewish thinking about resurrection. An elder named Razis was greatly upset

about the domination of the Greeks. Rather than fall into their hands, he decided to kill himself. Standing on a rock in front of a huge crowd, he took his sword and proceeded to disembowel himself. Second Maccabees 14:46 says that as he died he was "calling upon the Lord of life and spirit to give [his bodily parts] back to him again." Razis thought that by taking his own life he would escape this life to receive a new, better one.

(2) The Apocalypse of Baruch 50:2–51:10—Written between A.D. 70-100, the Apocalypse of Baruch expresses the same Jewish hope of resurrection. It says, "The earth shall then assuredly restore the dead, which it now receiveth in order to preserve them. It shall make no change in their form, but as it hath received, so shall it preserve them, and as it delivered them unto it, so shall it restore them. . . . For then it will be necessary to show to the living that the dead have come to life again, and that those who had departed have returned (again). . . . They shall respectively be transformed . . . into the splendour of angels . . . and time shall no longer age them. For in the heights of that world shall they dwell, and they shall be made like unto the angels, and be made equal to the stars, and they shall be changed into every form they desire, from beauty into loveliness and from light into the splendour of glory." That expresses the Jewish belief that, when you die, you will come to life in the same form in which you died.

(3) The Talmud—The Talmud is the codification of Jewish oral and written tradition. The resurrection of the body is a common teaching in the Talmud. It is one of the primary eschatological teachings of Judaism.

b) Biblical writings

God affirmed the truth of the resurrection in the Old Testament.

(1) Psalm 16:9-11—David said, "My heart is glad, and my glory rejoiceth; my flesh also shall rest in hope. For thou wilt not leave my soul in sheol, neither wilt thou permit thine Holy One to see corruption. Thou wilt show me the path of life." David's hope was that there would be no ultimate corruption or death but that eternal life would follow this life.

(2) Psalm 49:15—The psalmist said, "God will redeem my soul from the power of sheol; for he shall receive me."

(3) Psalm 73:24—The psalmist said, "Thou shalt guide me with thy counsel, and afterward receive me to glory."

(4) Hosea 6:1-2—Hosea said, "Come, and let us return unto the Lord; for he hath torn, and he will heal us; he hath smitten, and he will bind us up. After two days will he revive us, in the third day he will raise us up, and we shall live in his sight."

(5) Daniel 12:2—Daniel said, "Many of those who sleep in the dust of the earth shall awake, some to everlasting life, and some to shame and everlasting contempt." This is perhaps the clearest statement in the Old Testament concerning resurrection.

B. The Jewish Leaders in Particular

1. The major sects of Judaism

a) The Essenes

The Essenes were hermits who lived in the desert and spent most of their time copying scrolls. It is probable that they copied the famed Dead Sea Scrolls, which have been a major help in the study of ancient biblical manuscripts.

b) The Zealots

The Zealots were nationalistic political activists. They were terrorists who tried to end the Roman occupation of their land.

c) The Pharisees

The Pharisees were the religionists of their day. They held vigorously to an external, legalistic view in interpreting God's law. When they didn't want to follow the guidelines set forth in the law of Moses, they invented new standards to accommodate their sinfulness.

d) The Sadducees

Every one of the major sects of Judaism believed strongly in the resurrection of the body except the Sadducees.

2. The major tenets of the Sadducees

a) Their position

Every time the Sadducees are defined in Scripture, they are identified as disbelieving in resurrection. Luke declares in Acts 23:8, "The Sadducees say that there is no resurrection, neither angel, nor spirit; but the Pharisees confess both." They were in a continual theological debate with the Pharisees, who were more popular with the people because they believed in a resurrection.

b) Their power

Although the Sadducees were small in number, they were wealthy and influential. They were the aristocratic, ruling class. All the high priests and chief priests in Judaism were Sadducees. The majority of the members of the Sanhedrin—the ruling body in Israel—were Sadducees.

c) Their profits

The Sadducees were rich because they ruled all the buying and selling of merchandise in the Temple. They were unpopular because they gouged people with exorbitant rates in money changing. Also, they forced the people to buy high-priced Temple sacrifices instead of allowing them to bring their own sacrificial animals.

d) Their politics

The Sadducees were pro-Rome, which further added to their unpopularity. They supported Roman rule because they prospered under Roman tolerance. The Romans gave the Sadducees the right to operate as they saw fit. The people resented their courting Rome and chafed under their leadership.

e) Their passing

The Sadducees went completely out of existence in A.D. 70 when the Temple, the source of all their power, was destroyed. They could no longer profit from the people and therefore dropped from the scene.

f) Their preaching

(1) Their literal interpretation of the Scriptures

The Sadducees were very literal in interpreting the Scriptures. Josephus said that in rendering a judgment for the people, they were more vicious than any other sect of Judaism (*Antiquities* XX.ix.i). They were more narrow-minded and cruel than the Pharisees, who were more lenient in their application of the law. The Pharisees, in fact, frequently circumvented the law. For example, they permitted divorce in many situations.

The Sadducees refused the oral law, traditions, and scribal laws of the Pharisees. They refused everything but the Old Testament and gave primacy to the Pentateuch, the five books of Moses.

They prided themselves on guarding the pure faith of their ancestors.

(2) Their denial of the resurrection

The key focus of the Sadducees' doctrine was a rigid denial of the resurrection of the body. But if they believed the Old Testament, which in many places speaks of a resurrection, how could they deny the reality of a resurrection? Because they gave primacy to the Pentateuch. They thought the rest of Scripture merely commented on the five books of Moses. Since they didn't think the resurrection was taught in the five books of Moses, they didn't believe in it.

They believed that the body and soul went out of existence at death with no penalties and no rewards. Since they thought this life is all there is, they filled their lives with anything they could to fulfill their desires. Because they were limited by their strict, literal interpretation of the Scripture, they used their religion to justify license and gain profit.

The Sadducees mocked the Pharisees and confronted them continually about this particular issue. They would force them to come up with a verse from the Pentateuch that validated the resurrection. The Pharisees made a noble effort to respond, but they had a difficult time backing up their position. They usually cited the following to answer the Sadducees' claim that Moses never talked about resurrection.

(a) Numbers 18:28—Moses said, "Ye shall give thereof the Lord's heave offering to Aaron the priest." The Pharisees' reasoned that the verb is in the present tense and meant that Aaron had been resurrected. That, however, is a weak argument.

(b) Deuteronomy 31:16—Moses also said, "This people will rise up." That verse didn't convince the Sadducees either, because it was taken out of context.

(c) Deuteronomy 32:39—The Lord says, "I kill, and I make alive." But all that means is that God is the author of life and death. The Pharisees were stymied in their attempt to find a reference in the Pentateuch concerning the resurrection of the body.

Although the Pharisees and the Sadducees disagreed violently about the resurrection, Rome, and their social status, they agreed on one thing: the necessity of killing Jesus Christ. But why did the Sadducees desperately want to eliminate Jesus?

Lesson

I. THE APPROACH OF THE SADDUCEES (v. 23)

"The same day came to him the Sadducees, who say that there is no resurrection, and asked him."

A. Their Intent (v. 23a)

"The same day."

It was Wednesday of the week that our Lord was crucified. Jesus had been teaching in the Temple and was stopped by the religious leaders, who asked Him a series of questions. The first question came from the Pharisees and Herodians, who wanted to get Him in trouble with the Roman government. He answered their question in a marvelous way and indicted them instead (vv. 15-22). Verse 22 suggests that they abandoned their idea of getting Rome to execute Him for insurrection.

The Sadducees then came on the same day—Wednesday— with the intent of discrediting Him among the Jewish people. They wanted to make what He believed and taught appear foolish.

1. The hopelessness of the Sadducees

   What motivated the Sadducees to feel that way toward Jesus? The Sadducees had no real messianic hope because they did not believe in life after death. As far as they knew, they were living the good life in the here and now, because they were prospering with their Temple business. But the day before, Jesus had disrupted the Temple (Matt. 21:12-17). He had invaded their territory, and they wanted Him dead.

2. The hostility of the Sadducees

   The Sadducees watched on Monday as Jesus rode into the city and the people threw palm branches and garments at His feet. When the people hailed Him as the Son of David, Messiah, Savior, and King, they feared He would lead the nation into starting a riot that the Romans would have to stop. That would topple the delicate arrangement they had with the Romans.

   a) John 11:47-53—John said that at this time "gathered the chief priests and the Pharisees a council, and said, What do we? For this man doeth many miracles. If we let him thus alone, all men will believe on him; and the Romans shall come and take away both our place and nation. And one of them, named Caiaphas, being the high priest that same year, said unto them, Ye know nothing at all, nor consider that it is expedient for us that one man should die for the people, and that the whole nation perish not. And this spoke he not of himself; but, being high priest that year, he prophesied that Jesus should die for that nation; and not for that nation only, but that also he should gather together in one the children of God that were scattered abroad. Then from that day forth they took counsel together to put him to death." They were afraid Jesus would start a revolution that would affect their power, prestige, and wealth.

   b) Mark 14:1-2—Mark records, "After two days was the feast of the passover, and of the unleavened bread; and the chief priests and the scribes sought how they might take him by craft, and put him to death. But they said, not on the feast day, lest there be an uproar of the people." The Sadducees joined the Pharisees, their hated rivals, for mutual protection.

B. Their Indignation (v. 23*b*)

"The Sadducees, who say that there is no resurrection."

The Sadducees wholeheartedly rejected Jesus' teaching on the resurrection. They despised it not only because of their theology but also because of their godless life-style. If you want to live with disregard for the future, you don't want anyone teaching that you have to give an account of your present life in the next.

1. The hatred in the Sadducees

   a) Acts 4:1-2—As the disciples "spoke unto the people, the priests, and the captain of the temple, and the Sadducees, came upon them, being grieved that they taught the people, and preached through Jesus the resurrection from the dead."

   b) Acts 5:17, 28—"The high priest rose up, and all they that were with him (which is the sect of the Sadducees), and were filled with indignation . . . saying, Did not we strictly command you that ye should not teach in this name? And, behold, ye have filled Jerusalem with your doctrine, and intend to bring this man's blood upon us."

2. The hardening of the Sadducees

   The pressure was on the Sadducees because they knew the issue of resurrection would cause the crowds to turn against them. And if everyone began to believe in a resurrection, the Sadducees would be teaching doctrines no one listened to. The people did begin to turn away from the Sadducees and listen to Jesus and to the apostles after His earthly ministry. Josephus claims that the Sadducees were the ones who murdered James, the brother of the Lord (*Antiquities* XX.ix.i). So the Sadducees now attempted to discredit Jesus in front of the people.

II. THE SUPPOSED ABSURDITY OF THE RESURRECTION (vv. 24-28)

"Master, Moses said, If a man die, having no children, his brother shall marry his wife, and raise up seed unto his brother. Now there were with us seven brethren; and the first, when he had married a wife, died and, having no issue, left his wife unto his brother; likewise the second also, and the third, unto the seventh. And last of all the woman died also. Therefore, in the resurrection whose wife shall she be of the seven? For they all had her."

The Sadducees approached Jesus with what is called in Latin a *reductio ad absurdum*—a logical absurdity. They asked Jesus the same question they no doubt had asked the Pharisees on myriad occasions. By calling Jesus "Master," they were speaking condescendingly and flattering Him. John Broadus in his commentary on Matthew referred to this as "polished scoffing" ([Valley Forge: Judson, n.d.], p. 454).

A. The Levirate Law (v. 24)

"Moses said, If a man die, having no children, his brother shall marry his wife, and raise up seed unto his brother."

The Sadducees were referring to the Levirate law in the Mosaic covenant. The word comes from the Latin word *levir*, which means "husband's brother."

1. Deuteronomy 25:5-6—Moses said, "If brethren dwell together, and one of them die, and have no child, the wife of the dead shall not marry outside the family unto a stranger; her husband's brother shall go in unto her, and take her to him as his wife, and perform the duty of an husband's brother unto her. And it shall be, that the first-born whom she beareth shall succeed in the name of his brother who is dead, that his name be not put out of Israel." God gave this law to maintain the twelve tribes of Israel and the messianic line.

2. Genesis 38:8-10—Here we see the Levirate law applied before it was even given. Judah said to Onan, "Go in unto thy brother's wife, and marry her, and raise up seed to thy brother. And Onan knew that the seed

should not be his; and it came to pass, when he went in unto his brother's wife, that he spilled it on the ground, lest that he should give seed to the brother."

Onan refused to comply with God and raise up a child with his dead brother's wife, so God killed him (v. 10). God instituted that practice so that names and families could be passed on and the messianic line remain intact. The brother had to be single, however, because God did not command any polygamous relationships. The law was first given in patriarchal times to maintain the name, honor, and estate of a family.

3. Ruth 4:10—Boaz said, "Ruth, the Moabitess, the wife of Mahlon, have I purchased to be my wife, to raise up the name of the dead upon his inheritance, that the name of the dead be not cut off from among his brethren, and from the gate of his place."

Elimelech had two sons, and Ruth the Moabitess had married one of them. Both sons died, and there was no child to continue Elimelech's name or inheritance. Boaz took Ruth as his wife and raised up a child. God's providence clearly presided over this relationship because the line of Elimelech was the line of the coming Messiah of Israel. Boaz was a kinsman-redeemer. His taking the place of a dead husband and raising up a godly seed fit into the messianic line.

B. The Leading Question (vv. 25-28)

"Now there were with us seven brethren; and the first, when he had married a wife, died and, having no issue, left his wife unto his brother; likewise the second also, and the third, unto the seventh. And last of all the woman died also. Therefore, in the resurrection whose wife shall she be of the seven? For they all had her."

It is uncertain if the phrase "there were with us seven brethren" meant a personal acquaintance or a common illustration. Because the Pharisees taught that one would return in the same form and in the same clothes in which he died, the Sadducees demanded to know if the woman would then be the wife of all seven. If so, then you have polygamy in the eternal, resurrected state. This question must have stumped the Pharisees more often than they cared to acknowledge. The Sadducees must have thought they had Jesus in a bind because He, like the Pharisees, taught the reality of the resurrection of the body.

1. John 11:25-26—Jesus said, "I am the resurrection, and the life; he that believeth in me, though he were dead, yet shall he live. And whosoever liveth and believeth in me shall never die."

2. John 5:28-29—Jesus also said, "The hour is coming, in which all that are in the graves shall hear [My] voice, and shall come forth: they that have done good, unto the resurrection of life; and they that have done evil, unto the resurrection of damnation."

III. THE ANSWER OF SCRIPTURE (vv. 29-32)

"Jesus answered and said unto them, ye do err, not knowing the Scriptures, nor the power of God. For in the resurrection they neither marry, nor are given in marriage, but are like the angels of God in heaven. But as touching the resurrection of the dead, have ye not read that which was spoken unto you by God, saying, I am the God of Abraham, and the God of Isaac, and the God of Jacob? God is not the God of the dead, but of the living."

A. The Direct Approach (v. 29a)

"Jesus answered and said unto them, ye do err."

Jesus didn't vacillate in His response to the Sadducees. He in effect said, "You are wrong. You have just placed your ignorance on display." Commentator R. C. H. Lenski said, "The bubble blown by the folly of the Sadducees is punctured" (*The Interpretation of St. Matthew's Gospel* [Minneapolis: Augsburg, 1961], p. 871). The Greek word used for "err" is *planaō*, which means "to cause to wander" or "to lead astray." *Planaō* is the word used to derive the English word *planet*. The Greek word occurs in the middle reflexive voice, which means "you are causing yourself to wander" or "you are leading yourself astray from the truth."

1. Jude 13—Jude said false prophets are like "raging waves of the sea, foaming out their own shame; wandering stars, to whom is reserved the blackness of darkness forever." The Sadducees were much the same.

2. 1 Corinthians 15:35-42, 50-53—According to Paul, "Some man will say, How are the dead raised up? And with what body do they come? Thou fool, that which thou sowest is not made alive, except it die; and that which thou sowest, thou sowest not that body that shall be, but a bare grain, it may chance of wheat, or of some other grain. But God giveth it a body as it hath pleased him, and to every seed its own body. All flesh is not the same flesh, but there is one kind of flesh of men, another flesh of beasts, another of fish, and another of birds. There are also celestial bodies, and bodies terrestrial; but the glory of the celestial is one, and the glory of the terrestrial is another. There is one glory of the sun, and another glory of the moon, and another glory of the stars; for one star differeth from another star in glory. So also is the resurrection of the dead. It is sown in corruption; it is raised in incorruption. . . . Now this I say, brethren, that flesh and blood cannot inherit the kingdom of God; neither doth corruption inherit incorruption. Behold, I show you a mystery: We shall not all sleep, but we shall all be changed, in a moment, in the twinkling of an eye, at the last trump; for the trumpet shall sound, and the dead shall be raised incorruptible, and we shall be changed. For this corruptible must put on incorruption, and this mortal must put on immorality."

The apostle Paul had to deal with the same false teaching about the resurrection that Jesus did. The Corinthians were asking what kind of bodies they were going to have. Paul reminded them that God made different bodies. There are bodies of birds, creeping things, animals—terrestrial bodies—along with celestial bodies, those of mankind in the resurrection. God has one type of glory for the sun, one for the moon, and one for the stars. Everything that is made is different. Paul was telling the Corinthians not to think of God as being confined or limited. If He can produce variety here, infinite variety will be seen in the resurrection.

B. The Deadly Accusation (vv. 29b-32a)

1. The accusations in general (v. 29b)

"Not knowing the Scriptures, nor the power of God."

If there were two things the Sadducees thought they knew about, it was the Scriptures and the power of God. However, Jesus was saying, "You don't understand God's Word, and you don't understand God's power. Had you known the Scriptures, you would have known that God promises a resurrection. Had you known the power of God, you would have known that God wouldn't recreate people with the same problems as here on earth."

2. The accusations in specific (vv. 30-32a)

a) Ignorant of the power of God (v. 30)

"In the resurrection they neither marry, nor are given in marriage, but are like the angels of God in heaven."

The phrase "in the resurrection" simply refers to the state of life after death, or the experience of resurrection life. This verse does not say believers are angels but says they are *like* angels. We will be spiritual, eternal beings who will not marry or procreate in heaven. Why don't the angels procreate? Because they don't die, so there is no need to replace them. However, all humans die. Marriage and reproduction are necessary for the perpetuation of the race. They are for this life only. The Sadducees knew nothing of the power of God, who could create a body in the resurrection that would be greater than the one He created for this world. They had an inadequate view of God. Many Jewish teachers, including the famous medieval rabbi Maimonides, taught that there would be childbirth in the resurrection.

(1) Marriage is only for this life

There will be no marriages in the next life. That reality disappoints some people. However, others say, "Hallelujah! I have all the problems in marriage I can handle right now!" Some people are in a hurry to be married before the rapture because they're afraid they will miss something! In comparative terms, however, we need to realize that the best this life can offer, including marriage, can't begin to compare with the life to come. There will be no two people who have an exclusive, marital relationship in heaven. We will have a special relationship with everyone. Luke says in the parallel gospel account: "They are equal unto the angels, and are the sons of God, being the sons of the resurrection" (Luke 20:36). Man will be equal to the angels in the sense of equally free from death, equally spiritual, equally glorified, and equally eternal. Therefore there is no need to reproduce in heaven.

(2) Friendships are only for this life

This divine truth extends to friendships. No one will be closer to anyone else because all believers will be perfectly close to each other. And all believers will be perfectly intimate with the living God Himself.

b) Ignorant of the Scriptures (vv. 31-32a)

"As touching the resurrection of the dead, have ye not read that which was spoken unto you by God, saying, I am the God of Abraham, and the God of Isaac, and the God of Jacob?"

Jesus was saying they were ignorant even of the Pentateuch. When Jesus said, "Have ye not read?" He was being sarcastic, saying, "Haven't you been reading your own favored Scriptures about the resurrection?"

(1) Exodus 3:6—God said to Moses, "I am the God of thy father, the God of Abraham, the God of Isaac, and the God of Jacob." This, according to Jesus, is a statement about the resurrection. And He quoted from the Pentateuch because that was what the Sadducees demanded. The Greek verb *ego emi* in Matthew 22:32 is in the present tense and is the main argument of the passage. God doesn't say He *was* the God of Abraham, Isaac, and Jacob, but that He *is* their God. Abraham, Isaac, and Jacob were already dead physically at the time of the incident recorded in Exodus 3:6, but the verse implies that they were not dead.

(2) Genesis 26:24—The Lord appeared to Isaac and said, "I am the God of Abraham."

(3) Genesis 28:13—The Lord said to Jacob, "I am the Lord God of Abraham, thy father, and the God of Isaac."

C. The Decisive Answer (v. 32*b*)

"God is not the God of the dead, but of the living."

Since God says, "I am the God of Abraham, Isaac, and Jacob," they must be alive! God is not worshiped by corpses. He is not the God of people who don't exist.

1. The personal relationship

Why did God single out the patriarchal fathers by name, saying He is the God of Abraham, Isaac, and Jacob? To emphasize that He has a personal, intimate relationship with each one of them. The Greek use of the possessive phrase "the God of" could mean "the God to whom Abraham, Isaac, and Jacob belong" or "the God who belongs to Abraham, Isaac, and Jacob." I believe it is emphasizing both. God in effect is saying, "I am the God who continues to have a personal, intimate relationship with these men. They are mine, and I am theirs."

2. The permanent covenant

The eternal, unchanging, covenant-keeping God made promises to His chosen ones and will bring them to fulfillment. One day He will give them new bodies, yet even now they are enjoying fellowship with God.

Jesus devastated the Sadducees. He had done what the wisest rabbi had never been able to do. He had done what all the pharisaical masterminds could never do: showed the Sadducees passages right out of the Pentateuch to dispute their claims that there is no resurrection. Instead of making Jesus look foolish, the Sadducees succeeded only in making themselves look foolish. And they would soon see the most monumental resurrection of all: the resurrection of Jesus Christ Himself from the dead.

IV. THE ASTONISHMENT OF THE CROWD (v. 33)

"When the multitude heard this, they were astonished at his doctrine."

The Greek word translated "astonished" is *ekplessō*, which means "to strike out one's wits" (e.g., Matt. 7:28; 13:54). Luke adds that some of the scribes said, "Master, thou hast well said" (Luke 20:39). This new rabbi from Galilee had answered the supposedly unanswerable question and came up with a devastating argument that had been overlooked for centuries.

Conclusion

Jesus was confronted by hate-filled religious leaders who wanted Him dead. However, He was unaffected by their pecking assaults. They served only to manifest His greater glory and confound His enemies. Matthew 22:23-33 points to three great realities:

A. Christ's Majestic Deity

It is exciting to see Christ come up with answers no one else could come up with. Why? Because that proves Jesus is truly God in human flesh.

B. Christ's Commitment to Scripture

Jesus knew and loved the Word of God. He always had the right Scripture passage for the right situation. He put His entire confidence in the Word of God. And if Jesus relied on the Word, how much more should we?

C. Christ's Affirmation of the Resurrection

Whenever I am prone to doubt the resurrection, I am reminded that Jesus never doubted it for a moment. Our text affirms that believers who are dead physically are still alive because God is the God of the living.

Focusing on the Facts

1. What is the essence of everyone's future hope (see p. 35)?
2. What was Benjamin Franklin's view of death (see p. 36)?
3. What is the Talmud (see p. 37)?
4. Prove that the resurrection is taught in the Old Testament (see p. 38).
5. Name the four major sects of Judaism and explain each (see pp. 38-39).
6. True or false: The Essenes did not believe in the resurrection of the body (see p. 38).
7. What major sect of Judaism controlled both the Sanhedrin and priestly functions in Palestine (see p. 39)?
8. True or false: The Sadducees were much more popular with the Hebrew people than the Pharisees (see p. 39).
9. Why did the Sadducees go completely out of existence by the year A.D. 70 (see p. 40)?
10. What was the key focus of the Sadducees' doctrine (see pp. 41-42)?
11. What was the one issue the Pharisees and Sadducees agreed upon (see p. 42)?
12. What motivated the Sadducees to feel the way they did toward Jesus (see p. 43)?
13. What is the Levirate law? Explain your answer from Scripture (see pp. 45-46).
14. How did the apostle Paul deal with the question of resurrection (see p. 48)?

15. The two things the Sadducees were ignorant of were the
_____ and the _____ of
God (Matt. 22:29; see p. 49).
16. What does Matthew 22:30 teach us about what life in heaven
will be like (see p. 49)?
17. Explain the significance of God's saying, "I am the God of
Abraham, Isaac, and Jacob" (see p. 51).
18. Why did God single out the patriarchal fathers by name in saying, "I am the God of Abraham, Isaac, and Jacob" (Matt. 22:32;
see p. 51)?
19. Why was the multitude astonished at Jesus' doctrine (Matthew
22:33; see p. 52)?
20. To what three great realities does Matthew 22:23-33 point (see
pp. 52-53)?

Pondering the Principles

1. The skeptical Sadducees did not believe in the resurrection of
the dead. Many today are like them, thinking that when you
die, you simply go out of existence or sleep forever in the grave.
Based on your study of Matthew 22:23-33, is that true? Do you
believe in the resurrection of the dead? Read the following passages, and trust what the Word of God says about a future resurrection: Acts 26:6-8, 1 Thessalonians 4:14-16, and 2 Timothy
1:10.

2. Matthew 22:23-33 shows that Jesus Christ was truly God in human flesh. Do you believe that Jesus Christ is God? Can you lo-
cate other verses in Scripture that prove Christ's deity? Find
three passages, and then share your findings with others.

3
The Great Commandment

Outline

Introduction

Lesson
I. The Plot (v. 34)
   A. The Silence of the Sadducees
      1. Mark 1:25
      2. Mark 4:39
      3. 1 Corinthians 9:9
   B. The Struggle of the Pharisees
   C. The Summary of Scripture
      1. Psalm 2:2-3
      2. Acts 4:26-27
II. The Procedure (vv. 35-40)
   A. The Approach of the Pharisees (v. 35)
      1. The lawyer (v. 35a)
      2. The logic (v. 35b)
      3. The loyalty (v. 35c)
   B. The Question of the Lawyer (v. 36)
      1. The origin of Jewish law
      2. The obliteration of Jewish law
   C. The Response of the Lord (vv. 37-40)
      1. The command to love your God (vv. 37-38)
         a) The commitment of our love
            (1) "Heart"—intelligent love
            (2) "Soul"—emotional love
            (3) "Mind"—willing love
            (4) "Strength"—serving love
         b) The commitment of our Lord
            (1) John 15:13
            (2) Romans 5:8

Introduction

Someone has well said, "Love may not make the world go around, but it sure makes the trip worthwhile." That statement characterizes the universal sentiment that the sweetest of all human emotions is love. There are a vast number of songs, poems, books, stories, and films about love. God Himself would testify that the greatest of all possible human experiences is love. However, the kind of love God affirms is quite different from the kind of love the world understands. Matthew 22:34-40 is a passage about love, but it is not the normal type of human love. The passage is speaking about a love that only God can produce.

After two attempts at testing Jesus, the religious leaders again tried to discredit Him. The Pharisees and the Herodians first tried to test Him politically (vv. 15-22), followed by the Sadducees, who tried to test Him theologically (vv. 23-33). In Matthew 22:34-40, the Pharisees try once again, this time in the spiritual dimension. This was the last attempt of the religious leaders at questioning Jesus. Mark records that "no man after that dared to ask him any question" (Mark 12:34).

Lesson

I. THE PLOT (v. 34)

"When the Pharisees had heard that he had put the Sadducees to silence, they were gathered together."

A. The Silence of the Sadducees

The Greek verb for "to put to silence" is *ephimōsen*, which literally means "to be gagged." Jesus confounded the Sadducees. It wasn't that they wanted to be silent; they simply had no choice. The same Greek verb is used in many places in the New Testament.

1. Mark 1:25—Mark said, "Jesus rebuked him, saying, Hold thy peace, and come out of him." *Ephimōsen* is used here in reference to silencing a demon.

2. Mark 4:39—Jesus "rebuked the wind, and said unto the sea, Peace, be still. And the wind ceased, and there was a great calm." The verb is used here of the Lord's silencing a storm.

3. 1 Corinthians 9:9—Paul quoted Moses as saying, "Thou shalt not muzzle the mouth of the ox that treadeth out the grain." The verb is used here of muzzling an ox.

When *ephimōsen* is used in this way, it refers to an unwilling gagging. The Sadducees had more to say but nothing of real value to communicate. Jesus brought their argument to a complete end. They attempted to make Him look foolish, but He turned the tables on them.

B. The Struggle of the Pharisees

When the Pharisees heard of Jesus' interaction with the Sadducees, they must have had mixed emotions. They must have been glad to see their enemies silenced. They would have been happy to see the question answered, because they had probably grappled with it many times. However, they would much rather have seen Jesus discredited than the Sadducees silenced. There must have been a great deal of gloating over the Sadducees' ineptness, but that was far outweighed by their desire to destroy Jesus. He posed a far greater threat to them than the Sadducees ever would.

C. The Summary of Scripture

As the Pharisees gathered together, they became the fulfillment of prophecy.

1. Psalm 2:2-3—The psalmist said, "The kings of the earth set themselves, and the rulers take counsel together, against the Lord, and against his anointed, saying, Let us break their bands asunder, and cast away their cords from us."

2. Acts 4:26-27—Luke, quoting the psalmist, says, "The kings of the earth stood up, and the rulers were gathered together against the Lord, and against his Christ. For a truth against thy holy child, Jesus, whom thou hast anointed, both Herod, and Pontius Pilate, with the nations, and the people of Israel, were gathered together."

Psalm 2:2-3 looks to the cross and predicts a counsel of men plotting against Jesus. Acts 4:26-27 looks back at the cross and at all those gathered against Him. Even the plotting against Jesus fit into the plan of God as foretold in Scripture.

II. THE PROCEDURE (vv. 35-40)

"Then one of them, who was a lawyer, asked him a question, testing him, and saying, Master, which is the great commandment in the law? Jesus said unto him, Thou shalt love the Lord, thy God, with all thy heart, and with all thy soul, and with all thy mind. This is the first and great commandment. And the second is like it, Thou shalt love thy neighbor as thyself. On these two commandments hang all the law and the prophets."

A. The Approach of the Pharisees (v. 35)

"One of them, who was a lawyer, asked him a question, testing him."

1. The lawyer (v. 35a)

"One of them, who was a lawyer."

The Greek word translated "lawyer" refers to a legal expert. Matthew normally used the word translated "scribe" to refer to someone who was an expert in the law, but here he used a different word. Some Bible interpreters assume "lawyer" was not the word that Matthew intended to use because it is uncommon to his writing. But Matthew had the right to use any word he desired to communicate effectively. I believe he used that particular word to suggest that this particular Pharisee was a cut above the average scribe.

A scribe was one who copied the law and was an authority on interpreting the law. A scribe was half attorney, half theologian. He was an expert in biblical, not secular, law. The lawyer in verse 35 might have stood out as an expert among the experts. He was sent to Jesus to ask a question on behalf of the rest of the Pharisees.

2. The logic (v. 35b)

"Asked him [Jesus] a question."

The Pharisees were filled with hatred; all they wanted to do was eliminate Jesus Christ. The lawyer, however, seemed to be more objective than those who sent him. Mark's gospel describes the same scene and said, "One of the scribes came, and having heard them reasoning together, and perceiving that he had answered them well, asked him, Which is the first commandment of all?" (Mark 12:28). The lawyer thought Jesus had answered the Sadducees' question well. He was attracted to the wisdom of Jesus. He could easily play out his role as a Pharisee but could also get a direct answer that might help him in his own thinking. He was not totally innocent, because in verse 35 we read that he was tempting Jesus. Though not totally objective, he was nevertheless searching for the truth.

3. The loyalty (v. 35c)

"Testing him."

The primary authority in the history of Judaism has been Moses. Moses spoke to God face to face, as a man speaks to his friend, and that sets him apart from every other Jewish leader. God searched the world for a man through whom to give His law, and Moses was His choice. Moses penned the first five books of the Old Testament. He was and is the most admired man in Judaism. One rabbi said that since God called Moses faithful in all His house (Num. 12:6-7), that means He ranks Moses higher than the angels. Matthew 23:2 says, "The scribes and the Pharisees sit in Moses' seat," because that symbolized ultimate authority.

The Jewish leaders thought Jesus was attacking Moses' teaching. But Jesus said in the Sermon on the Mount that He did not come to destroy the law and the prophets but to fulfill them (Matt. 5:17). Jesus knew He would be accused of attacking Moses and setting up Himself as the new authority. The Pharisees were hoping Jesus would affirm that He went beyond Moses' teaching so they could accuse Him of being a heretic. If they could get Jesus to usurp Mosaic authority, He would become instantly unpopular with the people.

B. The Question of the Lawyer (v. 36)

"Master, which is the great commandment in the law?"

"Master" was a term the Jewish leaders used in the hopes of flattering Jesus and getting Him off guard. It refers to a teacher of the law. The lawyer's question was, "Which is the great commandment in the law?" The Greek text uses the word translated "great" as a comparative term, so the verse could be translated, "Which is the *greatest* commandment in the law?"

1. The origin of Jewish law

   The history of Jewish law records that there are 613 separate laws to be obeyed. The number was chosen because 613 separate letters are used in the Ten Commandments, and, as a result, the system is termed "rabbinical letterism." There is no other apparent connection between the letters and the laws. The Jews divided the law into two parts: 248 affirmative laws—one for every part of the human body—and 365 negative laws—one for every day of the year. They further subdivided them into light laws and heavy laws. The light laws were not as binding as the heavier laws. The Jews knew they couldn't possibly keep all 613 laws, so they were more lenient with some and heavy with others. Matthew 23:4 says the Pharisees "bind heavy burdens and grievous to be borne, and lay them on men's shoulders."

2. The obliteration of Jewish law

   There was much debate between the Jewish religious leaders on which laws were light and which were heavy. The Pharisees assumed Jesus was a man with a big ego who was trying to establish Himself as the Messiah. In their minds He was sure to set Himself up as the only authority. The Sadducees accepted only the Pentateuch and held Moses as their absolute authority. The Pharisees too held Moses as their supreme authority, but they also accepted the entire Old Testament as authoritative. They, as the Sadducees, expected Jesus to attempt to supersede Moses.

C. The Response of the Lord (vv. 37-40)

   "Jesus said unto him, Thou shalt love the Lord, thy God, with all thy heart, and with all thy soul, and with all thy mind. This is the first and great commandment. And the second is like it, Thou shalt love thy neighbor as thyself. On these two commandments hang all the law and the prophets."

1. The command to love your God (vv. 37-38)

"Thou shalt love the Lord, thy God, with all thy heart, and with all thy soul, and with all thy mind. This is the first and great commandment."

Jesus did the opposite of what the Pharisees expected Him to do: He quoted Moses directly from the Pentateuch (Deut. 6:5). He affirmed a strong solidarity with Mosaic teaching. Not only did He quote Moses, but He also quoted the most familiar passage Moses ever wrote. The *Shema* (Deut. 6:4-9; 11:13-21; Num. 15:37-41) was the most familiar Scripture to all Jews because they had to recite it twice a day. Every Jewish home had a *mezuza* by the front door with the Shema in it. The men strapped phylacteries (small boxes with portions of the Shema in them) to their foreheads and left arms to remind them of their responsibility to God. Many orthodox Jews follow the same practices today.

a) The commitment of our love

The Hebrew word for "love" in Deuteronomy 6:5 is *aheb*, which refers primarily to love exhibited by the will, mind, and actions rather than love exhibited by feelings or emotions. It is the highest kind of love, for it motivates you to do what is right and noble no matter what you may be feeling. It is akin to the *agapē* love of the Greek language, which is the love of intelligence, as opposed to *phileō*, which is the love of emotion, or *eros*, which is physical attraction. The love Jesus speaks of in the greatest commandment is the noblest, purest, and highest form of self-sacrificing love, which each person is commanded to have toward God.

The Jewish people already knew that the most important command was to love God with the whole heart, soul, mind, and—as Mark adds—strength (Mark 12:30). In pointing out all four aspects of human experience, Jesus was simply calling together all that a person is. He was saying, "You need to love God with your entire being." I don't think His intent was to emphasize the individual sense of each word, but there is something to be learned by studying the four words He used.

(1) "Heart"—intelligent love

The Hebrew understanding of the word *heart* refers to the core of one's being. Proverbs 4:23 says, "Keep thy heart with all diligence; for out of it are the issues of life." The heart is the intellect, which produces thoughts, words, and actions. Proverbs 23:7 says, "As he [man] thinketh in his heart, so is he." The intellectual part of a man is most often seen in the term *heart*, although the word is sometimes used to describe other aspects of human nature.

(2) "Soul"—emotional love

Matthew seems to use the word *soul* to refer to emotions. In Matthew 26:38 Jesus says, "My soul is exceedingly sorrowful."

(3) "Mind"—willing love

The Lord replaced the word *might* in Deuteronomy 6:5 with the word *mind*. He was not misquoting the verse because mind is simply another way of communicating might. The Greek word translated "might" is a broad word that has to do with the intention and will of a man. It refers to moving ahead with energy. The word *mind* can be used in the same sense.

(4) "Strength"—serving love

Mark adds the word *strength,* which refers to man's physical capacities. He is to love God even with all of his physical being.

There is a certain amount of overlapping in those words, but they form four channels of love in a perfect balance. We are commanded to love God with all the intellectual, emotional, volitional, and physical parts of our being.

b) The commitment of our Lord

God does not want people simply to go through religious rituals. God wants people to love Him with their entire beings. God expects no less than what He Himself offers, because He loves man with His whole being. He gave us Himself in death for our sin. Because He gave us His wholehearted love, He does not want halfhearted love in return. Since He loved us enough to give us His Son, we are to love Him enough to give Him ourselves.

(1) John 15:13—Jesus said, "Greater love hath no man than this, that a man lay down his life for his friends." We are to lay down our lives for God. That's what He did for us.

(2) Romans 5:8—Paul said, "God commendeth his love toward us in that, while we were yet sinners, Christ died for us." God showed that love can occur even where there is no initial reciprocation. We are to love God, not for what we gain, but because it is right to do so.

c) The commitment of our lives

Believing in God is not enough. He also wants us to obey Him. James 2:19 says, "The demons also believe, and tremble." Why then aren't they redeemed? Because even though they believe in God, they do not love or obey Him.

The distinguishing mark of any believer is that he loves God with all his heart and therefore obeys Him. God commands believers to love Him as much as they possibly can. Regardless of one's religious activity, no one is ever right with God until his heart, soul, mind, and strength manifest a love for God. A person does not prove he is a Christian simply because he believes in God. He demonstrates the validity of his faith when as a result of his belief, he displays a consuming love for God.

Even though the apostle Paul struggled in his Christian life, he loved God and hated sin. In Romans 7:18 he says, "I know that in me (that is, in my flesh) dwelleth no good thing; for to will is present with me, but how to perform that which is good I find not." Paul was saying he loved God with all his heart, even though he didn't always do the right thing. Even though he sometimes sinned, he nonetheless hated his sin. That is the mark of any Christian.

With this great commandment, Jesus unmasked the Pharisees and their hypocritical love for God. In fact He calls them hypocrites seven times in Matthew 23 (vv. 13-15, 23, 25, 27, 29). A hypocrite is someone who pretends to have something but really has nothing. The Pharisees did not love God with all their heart, soul, mind, and strength. They went through the religious motions, feeding their pride while trying to appear righteous.

d) The characteristics of obedience

The commandment Jesus spoke of was not new to the Pharisees. It was taken directly from Moses' writings and was a Mosaic way of describing redeemed people. Redeemed people are always characterized by obedience.

(1) Described in the Old Testament

(*a*) Exodus 20:6—The Lord said He shows His mercy to those who love Him and keep His commandments. God wanted the Pharisees to keep His commandments, but they couldn't because they didn't love Him.

(*b*) Deuteronomy 7:9—Moses said, "Know, therefore, that the Lord thy God, he is God, the faithful God who keepeth covenant and mercy with them who love him and keep his commandments."

(c) Nehemiah 1:5—Nehemiah said, "O Lord God of heaven, the great and awe-inspiring God, who keepeth covenant and mercy for them who love him and observe his commandments."

There was never a time or place in Old Testament times where God commanded external obedience apart from internal motivation. Obedience was always commanded from those who had willing hearts. Love is always the first step. When Jesus said to His disciples, "If ye love me, keep my commandments" (John 14:15), He wasn't saying anything new. God had been commanding that all along.

(2) Described in the New Testament

(a) 1 John 4:19—John said, "We love him, because he first loved us." Christians are those who love God.

(b) Ephesians 6:24—Paul said, "Grace be with all them that love our Lord Jesus Christ in sincerity." Grace is extended to those who honestly love the Lord.

e) The characteristics of disobedience

(1) 1 Corinthians 16:22—Paul said, "If any man love not the Lord Jesus Christ, let him be Anathema." God calls people to love Him.

(2) Exodus 20:5—In the Ten Commandments we read, "I, the Lord thy God, am a jealous God, visiting the iniquity of the fathers upon the children unto the third and fourth generations of them that hate me." Deuteronomy 5:9 reiterates the same idea.

(3) Deuteronomy 32:41—The Lord said, "I will render vengeance to mine enemies, and will reward them who hate me."

(4) Proverbs 8:36—According to Solomon, wisdom says, "He that sinneth against me wrongeth his own soul; all they that hate me love death."

It is basic for man to resent God, because He makes demands on our lives. If you don't love God, you hate Him. Jesus said, "He that is not with me is against me" (Matt. 12:30). The choice not to love God is an affront to His holy name, because He loved the world enough to send His Son to die on the cross for your sins. It is characteristic of the world to hate God.

The Love God Wants

God desires men to love Him. We express our love for Him by:

1. Meditating on God's glory (Ps. 18:1-3)
2. Trusting in God's great power (Ps. 31:23)
3. Seeking fellowship with God (Ps. 63:1-8)
4. Loving God's law (Ps. 119:165)
5. Being sensitive to how God feels (Ps. 69:9)
6. Loving what God loves (Ps. 119:72, 97, 103)
7. Loving whom God loves (1 John 5:1)
8. Hating what God hates (Ps. 97:10)
9. Grieving over sin (Matt. 26:75)
10. Rejecting the world (1 John 2:15)
11. Longing to be with Christ (2 Tim. 4:8)
12. Obeying God wholeheartedly (John 14:21)

Although the believer's obedience is imperfect, the love he has for God is still apparent. Paul says in Philippians 1:9, "I pray, that your love may abound yet more and more in knowledge." He was saying, "I know you love God, but I pray you learn to love Him more perfectly." A believer will love God throughout his life, yet there should be a continuing development of that reality. A true believer is a lover of God and a keeper of His commandments. Anyone who doesn't desire to keep God's commandments is someone who doesn't love Him or know Him.

f) The characteristics of forgiveness

Can men simply choose to stop hating God and start loving Him? No. It is impossible for man to generate this kind of love on his own because all men are bent toward hating God. The first step to loving God the way you should is to be forgiven of the hate you feel toward Him. The next step is to realize that you cannot forgive yourself, because you are incapable of atoning for your own sins. You need a Savior who can pay the penalty for your sin of not loving God.

(1) The need to love

Jesus Christ came into the world to die in your place and to pay the penalty for your sin of hating God. Man doesn't obey God and is indifferent to Him because he has never loved Him. Man needs to be forgiven for that. God wants to forgive man for this loveless attitude, and that's why Christ died on the cross. He bore the punishment for sin that we deserve to bear. Since we show we love God by obeying Him, we show we hate Him by disobeying Him.

(2) The ability to love

Christ not only can forgive man for a past lack of love but also can infuse man with the ability to love God in the present and future. Paul says in Romans 5:5, "The love of God is shed abroad in our hearts by the Holy Spirit." The Spirit of God, who indwells the believer at salvation, enables him to love God. We could never love God the way He desires, so we need divine enabling to do so. Jesus Christ came to pay the penalty for our sin. He forgives our unloving attitude toward God and enables us to love God through the indwelling Holy Spirit. When a believer sins, he hates his sin because he is controlled by his love for God.

That has always been God's standard. He wants people to love Him and keep His commandments. The Pharisees should have admitted they didn't really love God, evidenced by their inability to keep His commandments and their self-centered attitudes. They didn't ask for forgiveness because they didn't realize their complete lack of love for God. When you realize you don't really love God, Christ can come into your life, forgive your sin, and grant you the ability to love Him the way you should.

2. The command to love your neighbor (vv. 39-40)

"The second [commandment] is like it, Thou shalt love thy neighbor as thyself. On these two commandments hang all the law and the prophets."

The second commandment is like the first in that it is of the same nature and character. When you rightly love God, you will rightly love people. The Pharisees didn't love people. They bound heavy burdens on them (Matt. 23:4) and abused them. Their ancestors killed the prophets, and they were attempting to have Christ killed. They actually hated men; they stole their money and took bribes against people. They loved themselves more than they loved others.

a) The meaning (v. 39)

"The second is like it, Thou shalt love thy neighbor as thyself."

To love your neighbor as yourself means to love others with your whole heart. The love spoken of here is the same as that in the first commandment. It is the love of the will, intention, and action. The second commandment means to take care of someone else in the same way you would take care of yourself.

We are all concerned with our comfort and meeting our own needs. But are we as concerned with the comforts and needs of others? When you are hungry, you feed yourself, but when someone else is hungry, do you take care of him with the same concern? When you are uncomfortable, you find comfort. Do you have the same feeling for someone else who is in need of comfort? We need to care about others the same way we care about ourselves.

b) The message (v. 40)

"On these two commandments hang all the law and the prophets."

Christianity is not complicated. You simply love God and men with your entire being. If you love God, you'll do what He commands, and if you love men, you'll meet their needs. Verse 40 explains that these two commandments are behind all the other commandments in the Old Testament. If you love God with all your being and love everyone as you love yourself, you don't need any further rules. All the other commandments are simply an extension or practical application of those two commandments.

That there are laws in Scripture against murder indicates that people don't love each other. The same is true for laws in the Bible against idolatry. If we loved God the way we ought to, there would be no idols. Paul said, "He that loveth another hath fulfilled the law. For this, Thou shalt not commit adultery, thou shalt not kill, thou shalt not steal, thou shalt not bear false witness, thou shalt not covet; and if there be any other commandment, it is briefly comprehended in this saying, namely, Thou shalt love thy neighbor as thyself. Love worketh no ill to its neighbor; therefore, love is the fulfilling of the law" (Rom. 13:8-10). Everything reduces itself to loving God and your neighbor.

D. The Reaction of the Inquirer (Mark 12:32-34)

"The scribe said unto him, Well, Master, thou hast said the truth; for there is one God, and there is no other but he. And to love him with all the heart, and with all the understanding, and with all the soul, and with all the strength, and to love his neighbor as himself, is more than all whole burnt offerings and sacrifices. And when Jesus saw that he answered discreetly, he said unto him, Thou art not far from the kingdom of God. And no man after that dared to ask him any question."

The lawyer agreed with Jesus' words and then repeated what Jesus had said. Jesus replied, "Thou art not far from the kingdom of God." The lawyer's believing was good but not good enough. Believing is one step short of loving. God wants you to love Him by opening your heart and saying, "I want Jesus Christ to come into my life, forgive my unloving attitude, and enable me to love as I ought." Mark closes his description of this account by saying, "No man after that dared to ask him any question." They were no match for Jesus—and they knew it.

Conclusion

What is God calling for? He wants us to love Him, which is to obey Him, and to love our neighbors as ourselves. If you don't know Him, you need two things: a Savior to forgive you of your past, and divine enabling to help you love God in the present and future. If you are a Christian, you are already loving God and your neighbor, but you also recognize that sin hinders you from loving in the fullest sense. You need to starve the flesh and ask God to allow you to conquer sin. You will then begin to love Him and your neighbor more than ever before.

Believe It or Not!

Robert Ripley's "Believe It or Not!" says, "The longest—and simplest—love letter ever written was the work of a painter in Paris named Marcel de Leclure in 1875. The addressed was Magdalene de Villalore, his aristocratic light of love. The missive contained the phrase 'je vous aime' 'I love you' 1,875,000 times—a thousand times the calendar year of the date. The prodigious lover did not pen the letter with his own hand. He hired a scribe. A lazy type could have instructed the secretary: 'Write the amatory sentence 1,875,000 times.' But Leclure was too entranced with the sound of the three words. He dictated it word for word and had the hired man repeat it verbatim. All in all therefore the phrase was uttered orally and in writing 5,625,000 times—before it reached its destination. Never was love made manifest by as great an expenditure of time and effort" (cited in Paul Lee Tan's *Encyclopedia of 7,700 Illustrations* [Maryland: Assurance, 1980], pp. 755-56).

Ripley's thought is charming but false. Never was love made manifest by as great an expenditure of time and effort than when Christ died on the cross for man's sin. God's love for us is immeasurable. And when we return our whoiehearted love to God, we love Him even more than a man could love a woman. Likewise, we don't express our love to Him by writing, "I love you," more than a million times but by a life of obedience.

Focusing on the Facts

1. The sweetest of all human emotions is _____ (see p. 56).
2. What is the difference between the usual type of human love and the type of love Jesus speaks about in Matthew 22:34-40 (see p. 56)?
3. How did the Pharisees react to Jesus' silencing of the Sadducees (see pp. 56-57)?
4. How did the Pharisees fulfill prophecy when they questioned Jesus (see p. 58)?
5. What is the definition of a scribe, and why might Matthew have used a different word to describe the lawyer (see p. 59)?
6. What was different about that particular lawyer and the rest of the Pharisees (see p. 59)?
7. True or false: The primary authority in the history of Judaism has been Moses (see p. 60).
8. What did the Jewish leaders believe about Jesus' teaching (see p. 60)?
9. Why did the Jewish people conclude that Scripture gives 613 separate laws to obey? Is their method of arriving at that conclusion valid (see p. 61)?
10. Did Jesus respond the way the Jewish leaders wanted Him to? How did He respond to the lawyer's question (see p. 62)?
11. What is the meaning of the word *love* in Deuteronomy 6:5? What is its equivalent in the Greek language (see p. 62)?
12. The love Jesus speaks of in the greatest commandment is the _____, _____, and _____ form of self-sacrificing love that each person is commanded to have toward God (see p. 62).

13. What are the four aspects of loving God? Explain each (see p. 63).
14. What is the distinguishing mark of the Christian (see p. 64)?
15. What is the definition of a hypocrite? Why were the Pharisees seen by Jesus as hypocritical (see p. 65)?
16. Redeemed people are always characterized by _____ (see p. 65).
17. True or false: There was a time when God commanded externally motivated obedience apart from internal motivation (see p. 66).
18. Describe the love that God wants (see p. 67).
19. What is the first step in loving God the way you should? What is the next step (see p. 68)?
20. What is second great commandment, and how is it like the first (see p. 69)?
21. What is the message of Matthew 22:40 (see p. 70)?
22. What is God calling for in Matthew 22:37-40? If someone is deficient in those areas, what should he do (see p. 71)?
23. We do not express our love to God by writing, "I love you," more than a million times but by a life of _____ (see p. 72).

Pondering the Principles

1. When asked in Matthew 22:36, "Which is the greatest commandment?" Jesus responds, "Thou shalt love the Lord, thy God, with all thy heart, and with all thy soul, and with all thy mind." Man is commanded to love God with his entire being. Do you love God with all your heart, soul, mind, and strength? If your answer is no, ask God to allow you to love Him as you should. Focus on the twelve points describing the love God wants (see p. 67). Take one a month, and ask God to make it a reality in your life for that month.

2. The greatest commandment would be incomplete without the second, "Thou shalt love thy neighbor as thyself." That allows us to channel God's love to others. Do you love others as much as you love yourself? When they have needs, do you seek to meet theirs before your own? Memorize Philippians 2:3-5, and begin to love others as you love yourself.

4
Whose Son Is Christ?

Outline

Introduction
A. The Descriptions of Jesus Christ
B. The Denials of Jesus Christ

Lesson
I. The Incisive Question (vv. 41-42*a*)
  A. The Tables Are Turned (v. 41*a*)
    1. The indictment
    2. The invitation
  B. The Question Is Asked (vv. 41*b*-42*a*)
    1. The indirectness
    2. The importance
II. The Inadequate Answer (v. 42*b*)
  A. The Scribal Teaching
    1. The Old Testament
    2. The New Testament
  B. The Davidic Tracing
    1. The pattern
    2. The problem
  C. The Partial Truth
III. The Infinite Reality (vv. 43-45)
  A. The Significance (v. 43)
    1. Genesis 15:1-2
    2. Deuteronomy 10:17
    3. Psalm 35:23
    4. Psalm 38:15
    5. Malachi 1:6
  B. The Spirit (v. 43*b*)

C. The Scripture (v. 44)
   1. The intent (v. 44*a*)
      a) Psalm 110 is messianic
      b) Psalm 110 is written by David
      c) Psalm 110 affirms the deity of Messiah
   2. The rank (v. 44*b*)
      a) The symbol
      b) The subjugation
         (1) Joshua 10:24-25
         (2) Psalm 2:7-9
D. The Sarcasm (v. 45)
   1. The doctrine
      a) The humanity of Jesus
         (1) Luke 2:52
         (2) Matthew 26:38
      b) The deity of Jesus
         (1) Matthew 18:20
         (2) Romans 1:3
         (3) 2 Timothy 2:8
         (4) Philippians 2:6-10
         (5) John 1:14
   2. The determination
IV. The Inappropriate Response (v. 46)
  A. Of the Crowd
  B. Of the Pharisees

Conclusion

Introduction

A. The Descriptions of Jesus Christ

The most important of all questions is, Who is Jesus Christ? When it comes to opinions about Jesus Christ, the world has never lacked ideas.

1. By ancient Jewish leaders

According to the Talmud, the Jewish leaders said Jesus practiced magic and led Israel astray (*Sanhedrin* 43*a*). That comment was written somewhere between A.D. 100 and A.D. 200. Many have taken a strong, negative view of Jesus. The Jewish leaders of Jesus' own day said He performed miracles by the power of the devil himself (Matt. 12:24).

2. By Julian the Apostate

Julian the Apostate, Roman emperor from A.D. 361-363, said, "Jesus has now been celebrated about three hundred years; having done nothing in his lifetime worthy of fame, unless any one thinks it a very great work to heal lame and blind people and exorcise demoniacs in the villages of Bethsaida and Bethany" (quoted by Cyril, fifth-century bishop of Alexandria, in *Contra Julian*, lib. vi., p. 191).

3. By Jean-Jacques Rousseau

Humanity has generally been condescending and complimentary toward Jesus. French philosopher Jean-Jacques Rousseau said, "When Plato describes his imaginary righteous man loaded with all the punishments of guilt, yet meriting the highest rewards of virtue, he describes exactly the character of Jesus Christ. . . . The life and death of Jesus are those of a God" (*Oeuvres complètes* [Paris, 1839], tome iii, pp. 365-67).

4. By Ralph Waldo Emerson

Although not believed to be a Christian, this famous poet said that Jesus is the most perfect of all the men that have yet appeared on the earth (*The Collected Works of Ralph Waldo Emerson*, vol. 1 [Cambridge, Mass.: Harvard, 1971], p. 80).

5. By Napoleon

Napoleon said, "I know men, and I tell you that Jesus Christ was not a man" (*Law, Love and Religion of Napoleon Bonaparte in His Own Words*, ed. Hiram E. Casey [New York: Carlton, 1961], p. 64).

6. By John Stuart Mill

English philosopher and economist John Stuart Mill said Jesus was "the pattern of perfection for humanity" (*Three Essays on Religion* [New York: Holt, reprint of 1874 ed.], p. 253).

7. By William E. Lecky

Irish historian and essayist William E. Lecky said Jesus was "the highest pattern of virtue" (*History of European Morals from Augustus to Charlemagne* [New York: D. Appleton, 1903], p. 8).

8. By Ernest Renan

French philologist and historian Ernest Renan said Jesus "will never be surpassed" (*The Life of Jesus* [New York: Modern Library, 1864], p. 376).

9. By Theodore Parker

American Unitarian clergyman Theodore Parker called Jesus the youth with God in His heart (*A Discourse of Matters Pertaining to Religion* [Boston: Rufus Leighton, 1859], p. 281).

10. By David Strauss

German theologian and philosopher David Strauss, a staunch critic of Christianity, said Jesus is "the highest model of religion within the reach of [human] thought" (*Vergängliches und Bleibendes im Christenthum* [Freihafen: 1838], p. 47).

11. By H. G. Wells

English novelist H. G. Wells wrote, "When I was asked which single individual has left the most permanent impression on the world, the manner of the questioner almost carried the implication that it was Jesus of Nazareth. I agreed. . . . Jesus stands first" ("The Three Greatest Men in History," *Reader's Digest* [May 1935]:12-14).

Even many who don't believe in Jesus Christ have stated that He was the best of men.

B. The Denials of Jesus Christ

Underneath those complimentary descriptions of Jesus Christ is an incipient denial that He was anything more than the best man among men. Christianity has always found its most violent detractors and aggressive attackers at its doctrinal core: the deity of Jesus Christ. Christ's deity is attacked more than any other Christian doctrine. The major emphasis in denying the deity of Jesus Christ is that He was a man and nothing more.

1. By the Christadelphians

An advertisement said, "Sunday at 7 P.M., the Christadelphians invite you to a Bible address on the subject, 'Jesus is not God,' given by Arthur Woods, Bible teacher/lecturer."

2. By liberal Protestantism

On January 21, 1984, the *Seattle Times* ran a feature article entitled "Jesus as Man." It said, "The Rev. David Aasen, pastor of the First United Methodist Church . . . has swung vigorously into a sermon series emphasizing Jesus Christ as man, not God." He said the reason there is any controversy at all concerning this issue is "there's always a bunch of people who say Jesus is God." He said further that it is important "for us to have as proper a perspective of Jesus as we can . . . to know Jesus as he really is and not some, ah, fantasy." His associate, Rev. Gary Starkey, said, "Jesus is one of us." The article suggested that Jesus was merely like a Mother Teresa or Caesar Chavez.

3. By the Anthroposophical Society

The Anthroposophical Society, which was founded by Rudolph Steiner, teaches that Jesus was an ordinary man who at thirty received the Christ's essence.

4. By Islam

Muslim theology teaches that Jesus was a prophet but not the equal of Mohammed.

5. By Christian Science

Christian Scientists teach that Jesus was a mere man who lived out a divine ideal but that His blood cleanses nothing.

6. By The Church of the Living Word

The Church of the Living Word's leader, John Robert Stevens, considers himself to be God's chief apostle and intercessor.

7. By The Church Universal and Triumphant

Elizabeth Claire Prophet, their leader, says that Jesus was a man with Christ consciousness but only one of many men who have achieved that level.

8. By Freemasonry

Hertel's Bible, the Masons' edition of the Bible, says, "We tell the sincere Christian that Jesus of Nazareth was but a man like us" (p. 9).

9. By the Hare Krishnas

Devotees of Hare Krishna believe that Jesus is just another guru.

10. By the I Am (Ascended Masters) movement

This group believes Jesus is an ascended master.

11. By the Jehovah's Witnesses

The Jehovah's Witnesses teach that Jesus Christ is the created being Michael.

12. By the Mormons

   The Mormons believe Jesus is the spirit brother of Lucifer.

13. By Rosicrucianism

   The Rosicrucian religion identifies Jesus Christ as a reincarnate cosmic man.

14. By Scientology

   Scientology teaches that Christ achieved a clear state (freedom from problems or difficulties—no neuroses or illnesses) but not the highest state of a "Thetan" (an immortal spirit).

15. By The Local Church

   The Local Church, led by Witness Lee, says that Christ was neither God nor man but a mixture of the two.

16. By The Unification Church

   Sun Myung Moon believes Christ must achieve perfection by marrying and having perfect babies.

17. By The Way International

   The Way International denies that Jesus Christ is God.

18. By the Unitarians

   The Unitarians teach that Christ was only a man.

Those are but a few of myriad attacks on Christ's deity—the doctrine where the main battle lines are drawn for the Christian faith. Misrepresentations and misconceptions are not new to Christianity. Matthew 22:41-46 describes another group of people who denied the deity of Jesus Christ. The Jewish leaders believed the Messiah would be a military leader and certainly not God in human flesh. Jesus was now to correct that serious error.

Lesson

I. THE INCISIVE QUESTION (vv. 41-42*a*)

"While the Pharisees were gathered together, Jesus asked them, saying, What think ye of Christ? Whose son is he?"

A. The Tables Are Turned (v. 41*a*)

"While the Pharisees were gathered together."

The Pharisees and Herodians had asked Jesus a question, and He answered them beautifully (vv. 15-22). The Sadducees came and asked Him another question, and He answered that (vv. 23-33). The Pharisees regrouped and came with yet another question (vv. 34-40). Although Jesus had answered all His critics, the Pharisees were still gathered together in a last-ditch effort to discredit Him. The problem was they had no more questions to ask. They had no more weapons left because their arsenal was depleted. So Jesus turned the tables on the Pharisees and asked them a question. His confrontation was twofold.

1. The indictment

Jesus' clear proclamation of who He is was an indictment against their ignorance. They assumed the Messiah would be only a man. Jesus proved from their own Scriptures that the Messiah is also God. The Jewish leaders had asked Jesus by whose authority He taught (Matt. 21:23). In Matthew 22:41-46, He answers their question. Jesus' authority was His own because He was God.

2. The invitation

Jesus also extended an invitation to some of the Pharisees, because not all of them were as rigid in their rejection of Him (Mark 12:34). There must have been some who were close to salvation. Further information about the deity of Christ could bring them into the kingdom.

B. The Question Is Asked (vv. 41b-42a)

"Jesus asked them, saying, What think ye of Christ? Whose son is he?"

1. The indirectness

Jesus asked the Pharisees, "What is your opinion of the Christ?" He did not ask about Himself. That would have been too direct. *Christos* is a New Testament term for the Old Testament term *Messiah*. Jesus wanted to know whose son they thought the Messiah was.

2. The importance

That question must have appeared simple to those learned Jewish leaders, but only because they didn't know the full answer. Since they never understood the fullness of what the Messiah's role would be, they never understood His true identity. They thought the Messiah's role was merely political. Jesus wanted to take them to a higher understanding.

II. THE INADEQUATE ANSWER (v. 42b)

"They say unto him, The Son of David."

A. The Scribal Teaching

The Pharisees hurried to show Jesus their knowledge but instead showed their ignorance. Any Jewish person would have given the same reply, because that was the standard scribal teaching concerning the Messiah (Mark 12:35). The scribes got their information from the Old Testament.

1. The Old Testament

a) 2 Samuel 7:12-13—The Lord said to David, "When thy days be fulfilled, and thou shalt sleep with thy fathers, I will set up thy seed after thee, which shall proceed out of thine own body, and I will establish his kingdom. He shall build an house for my name, and I will establish the throne of his kingdom forever." That could not refer to King Solomon because his kingdom didn't last forever. The prophecy was saying that from the seed of David would come one who would have an eternal kingdom. From the time of prophecy onward, the Jewish people referred to that particular Son of David as the Messiah, which means "the anointed one."

b) Psalm 89:3-4, 20-21, 24, 34-37—The psalmist said, "I have made a covenant with my chosen, I have sworn unto David, my servant: Thy seed will I establish forever, and build up thy throne to all generations. . . . I have found David, my servant; with my holy oil have I anointed him, with whom my hand shall be established; mine arm also shall strengthen him. . . . My faithfulness and my mercy shall be with him; and in my name shall his horn be exalted. . . . My covenant will I not break, nor will I alter the thing that is gone out of my lips. Once have I sworn by my holiness that I will not lie unto David. His seed shall endure forever, and his throne as the sun before me. It shall be established forever like the moon, and as a faithful witness in heaven." God promised that David's Son, the anointed one, would reign in an eternal kingdom.

c) Amos 9:11—The Lord said, "In that day will I raise up the tabernacle of David that is fallen, and close up the breaches of it; and I will raise up his ruins, and I will build it as in the days of old."

d) Micah 5:2—Micah said, "Thou, Bethlehem Ephrathah, though thou be little among the thousands of Judah, yet out of thee shall he come forth unto me that is to be ruler in Israel, whose goings forth have been from of old, from everlasting."

e) Ezekiel 37:24-27—As Ezekiel looked to the millennial kingdom he said, "David, my servant, shall be king over them, and they all shall have one shepherd; they shall also walk in mine ordinances, and observe my statutes, and do them. And they shall dwell in the land that I have given unto Jacob my servant, in which your fathers have dwelt; and they shall dwell in it, even they, and their children, and their children's children forever; and my servant, David, shall be their prince forever. Moreover, I will make a covenant of peace with them; it shall be an everlasting covenant with them; and I will place them, and multiply them, and will set my sanctuary in the midst of them for evermore. My tabernacle also shall be with them; yea, I will be their God, and they shall be my people."

Beginning in the millennial kingdom and stretching into eternity, David's greater Son—the Lord Jesus Christ Himself—will rule an everlasting kingdom. The Jewish leaders knew that the Messiah was to be of the seed of David.

2. The New Testament

a) Matthew 9:27—Two blind men cried out to Jesus, "Thou Son of David, have mercy on us."

b) Matthew 12:23—When Jesus healed a demoniac, all the people said, "Is not this the son of David?"

c) Matthew 15:22—A woman from Canaan cried out to Jesus, saying, "Have mercy on me, O Lord, thou Son of David."

d) Matthew 20:30—Two more blind men said, "Have mercy on us, O Lord, thou Son of David."

e) Matthew 21:9—The multitudes said, "Hosanna to the Son of David! Blessed is he that cometh in the name of the Lord!"

f) Matthew 21:15—When Jesus cleansed the Temple, the children shouted, "Hosanna to the Son of David!"

B. The Davidic Tracing

1. The pattern

Since everyone knew the Messiah would come from the lineage of David, Matthew went into great detail to present the genealogy of Jesus Christ. He began his gospel by saying, "The book of the genealogy of Jesus Christ, the son of David, the son of Abraham." He then traced Christ's genealogy all the way down to Joseph. Luke followed the same pattern, although he traced the Messiah through the line of Mary (1:27, 32-33). Jesus Christ was indeed a son of David because both His earthly father and mother were in the Davidic family.

2. The problem

If Jesus had not been in the Davidic line, you can be sure that the Pharisees would have made that a major issue. They would have disqualified Jesus instantly from any claim of being the Messiah. They kept Temple records of every Jewish person's genealogy and therefore would have known if Jesus did not come from David's line. Those records were kept until the destruction of the Temple in A.D. 70. Jewish people today no longer know the tribe to which they belong, because the records have all been lost. However, no Jewish person in Jesus' time could hold any civic office unless his genealogy was known. A priest would never marry someone whose genealogy he did not know. That the Pharisees never questioned Jesus' heritage indicates He was from the line of David. He was, therefore, humanly qualified to be the king of Israel. Had the monarchy still existed, He would have been king.

C. The Partial Truth

As right as the Pharisees' answer was, it was still only partially true. In answering Jesus' question, the Pharisees may have been in effect saying, "Why are you letting people call you the Son of David? That messianic title is too great to refer to you." Jesus responded by saying, "No, that messianic title is actually too small a title for Me. David had many descendants, but I am the greatest of those." In the minds of the Pharisees, that raised the question of how Jesus could be greater than all of David's descendants, including the great King Solomon and the prophet Hezekiah. They thought the Messiah would be someone far more impressive than Jesus of Nazareth.

III. THE INFINITE REALITY (vv. 43-45)

"He saith unto them, How, then, doth David, in the Spirit, call him Lord, saying, The Lord said unto my Lord, Sit thou on my right hand, till I make thine enemies thy footstool? If David, then, calls him Lord, how is he his son?"

The Lord responded to the Pharisees' inadequate answer by presenting them with a marvelous truth. It is a divine exposition of Psalm 110:1 by the Lord Himself.

A. The Significance (v. 43)

"He saith unto them, How, then, doth David, in the Spirit, call him Lord?"

Jesus responded to the Pharisees by first saying that David called the Messiah "Lord." The Greek word for "Lord" is *kurios* and is a common word in the New Testament. It is most often used for describing the deity of Jesus Christ. The Hebrew word for "Lord" in the Old Testament is *adonai*, a title for God. Note the following examples:

1. Genesis 15:1-2—"The word of the Lord came unto Abram in a vision, saying, Fear not, Abram: I am thy shield, and thy exceedingly great reward. And Abram said, Lord God . . ."

2. Deuteronomy 10:17—Moses said to the Israelites, "The Lord your God is God of gods, and Lord of lords."

3. Psalm 35:23—David said to God, "Stir up thyself, and awake to my right, even unto my cause, my God and my Lord."

4. Psalm 38:15—David said, "In thee, O Lord, do I hope; thou wilt hear, O Lord, my God."

5. Malachi 1:6—The Lord said, "A son honoreth his father, and a servant his master; if, then, I be a father, where is mine honor? And if I be a master, where is my fear? saith the Lord of hosts unto you."

Jesus asked the Pharisees an important question: "If the Messiah was only David's human son, how is it that David called Him Lord, a term that refers to God?"

B. The Spirit (v. 43b)

"How, then, doth David, in the Spirit, call him Lord?"

The Pharisees could have thought King David made a mistake in calling the Messiah Lord. Maybe they thought David was giving only his own opinion or that this wasn't even David speaking at all. However, Jesus made the Pharisees absolutely certain by stating that David was "in the Spirit" when he called the Messiah Lord.

The phrase "in the Spirit" refers to being under the control of the Holy Spirit (Rev. 1:10; 4:2). There is no doubt Jesus was referring to the Holy Spirit, because Mark's gospel gives Jesus' entire statement: "David himself said, by the Holy Spirit, The Lord said to my Lord" (Mark 12:36). Jesus was not speaking of David's human spirit, but about the Holy Spirit. King David was under divine inspiration when he called the Messiah *adonai*, thus calling Him God.

C. The Scripture (v. 44)

"The Lord said unto my Lord, Sit thou on my right hand, till I make thine enemies thy footstool."

In verse 44 Jesus cites the exact statement of David from Psalm 110:1: "The Lord [*elohim*] said unto my Lord [*adonai*]." There you have two Lords speaking to each other.

1. The intent (v. 44a)

"The Lord said unto my Lord."

Jesus used Psalm 110:1 for many reasons but chiefly because all Jewish people believed it was a messianic psalm. They didn't understand the full implications of the first verse but nevertheless believed it to be messianic. Psalm 110 is the most frequently quoted psalm in the New Testament. It is quoted by Peter (Acts 2:34-35), Paul (1 Cor. 15:25), and the writer of Hebrews (1:13;

10:13). It is quoted in the gospels of Matthew, Mark, and Luke. In all three gospels Jesus attributed it to David.

a) Psalm 110 is messianic

The Lord Jesus Himself affirmed the messianic character of Psalm 110.

b) Psalm 110 is written by David

Although you don't see David's name in Psalm 110, Jesus knew David wrote it. It was traditionally ascribed to David by the Jews, and Jesus confirmed that tradition.

c) Psalm 110 affirms the deity of Messiah

The main reason Jesus used Psalm 110 was to affirm the deity of the Messiah. The intent of Matthew 22:41-46 was to affirm to the Pharisees and to the world that the Messiah—Jesus Himself—is God incarnate and affirmed as such by King David.

The Denial of the Critics

I was amazed to find while reading commentaries dealing with Matthew 22:41-46 that many deny the messianic and prophetic character of Psalm 110. They don't believe the Bible is a supernatural book and therefore assume it can't predict the future; they look at it as only a historical document.

Some scholars contend that David's language could not have been as developed as it is in Psalm 110, saying that the rich expressions in Psalm 110 would require it to have been written much later than David's time. They also cite that the priest/king relationship in the psalm (v. 4) would have been totally unfamiliar to David. Not necessarily, however. Priests, kings, and rich literary expressions existed at and before David's time.

We know David wrote Psalm 110 under the inspiration of the Holy Spirit, because Jesus Himself said so. So when critics deny the messianic and prophetic character of Psalm 110, they are denying the deity of Jesus Christ or calling Him a liar. To do that is to ignore the evidence of who He really is.

2. The rank (v. 44*b*)

"Sit thou on my right hand, till I make thine enemies thy footstool."

God the Father has given the Messiah a position that brings Him into a co-equal place of power and authority with Himself. God Himself declares the Messiah's deity. Hebrews 1:3 declares that Jesus, "being the brightness of his glory, and the express image of his person, and upholding all things by the word of his power, when he had by himself purged our sins, sat down on the right hand of the Majesty on high." Equal glory was promised to the Messiah, because He is equal to God.

a) The symbol

The phrase "sit thou on my right hand" is a symbol of authority because the right hand represents strength and power. Likewise, Christ was put at the right hand of God to symbolize a place of equality, authority, and power. The Greek text of Matthew 22:44 literally says, "Be thou sitting," which is in the continuous imperative tense and means, "Take a continuous place of exaltation on the right hand of God."

b) The subjugation

The authority and power of the Messiah's rule are invincible. Verse 44 quotes Psalm 110:1 as saying, "Till I make thine enemies thy footstool." God was in effect saying, "Messiah! I will subjugate everything under You. All Your enemies will ultimately become Your footstool." That pictures the ancient Oriental practice of a king's putting his heel on the neck of his vanquished foe.

(1) Joshua 10:24-25—Joshua said to his men regarding their captives, "Come near, put your feet upon the necks of these kings. And they came near, and put their feet upon the necks of them. And Joshua said unto them . . . Thus shall the Lord do to all your enemies against whom ye fight."

(2) Psalm 2:7-9—David writes from the Messiah's perspective, "I will declare the decree: The Lord hath said unto me, Thou art my Son; this day have I begotten thee. Ask of me, and I shall give thee the nations for thine inheritance, and the uttermost parts of the earth for thy possession. Thou shalt break them with a rod of iron; thou shalt dash them in pieces like a potter's vessel."

D. The Sarcasm (v. 45)

"If David, then, call him, Lord, how is he his son?"

The Pharisees responded to Jesus by saying the Messiah was the son of David, but that was not enough. He is also the Son of God. Verses 43-45 are a riddle the Pharisees couldn't answer. They were the religious leaders of Israel, yet they were stumped. The main trust of Judaism could not answer Him, because they would not acknowledge Jesus as God and man. The Pharisees no doubt asked themselves, *How can the Messiah be the son of David and David's Lord at the same time? He would have to be God and man.* They knew Jesus was the son of David because they surely would have checked His genealogy. But they also had overwhelming evidence that He was the Son of God. The Pharisees had to fight the obvious to conclude anything other than that.

The apostle John wrote, "There are also many other things which Jesus did, which, if they should be written every one. . . . the world itself could not contain the books that should be written" (John 21:25). All the healings, miracles, resurrections, and divine teaching demonstrated that He was the Son of God. However, instead of acknowledging His deity, the Pharisees refused to utter a word.

1. The doctrine

The heart of Christianity is that Jesus Christ is both God and man. The Scripture is abundantly clear about the humanity and the deity of Christ. If nothing else in the Bible declared the humanity and deity of Christ, Revelation 22:16 would be enough: "I, Jesus, have sent mine angel to testify unto you these things in the churches. I am the root and the offspring of David." Jesus is David's Son and his Lord at the same time. He is the God-man.

a) The humanity of Jesus

(1) Luke 2:52—Jesus, as any other human being, "increased in wisdom and stature, and in favor with God and man." He knew pain, thirst, hunger, weariness, sleep, pleasure, and death.

(2) Matthew 26:38—Jesus said, "My soul is exceedingly sorrowful, even unto death." He had feelings (Isa. 53:3; John 13:21). He is called the Son of man (Acts 7:56) and the man Christ Jesus (1 Tim. 2:5). He possessed flesh and blood (Heb. 2:14; 1 John 4:2-3). He could be touched and embraced. His feet could be kissed and washed, and His beard could be plucked. He was crowned with a crown of thorns and nailed to a cross. A spear was thrust into His side. He was tempted as we are but without sin (Heb. 4:15). He was David's human offspring.

b) The deity of Jesus

(1) Matthew 18:20—Jesus said, "Where two or three are gathered together in my name, there am I in the midst of them." He is omnipresent.

He is also omnipotent (Matt. 28:18), the Creator and commander of all the elements (Col. 1:16). He is the forgiver of sin and judge of the universe (Acts 10:42). He is omniscient (Col. 2:3) and unchanging (Heb. 13:8).

He demonstrated in His earthly life that He, as God, is holy (Luke 1:35), true (Zech. 9:9), and sovereign (Heb. 1:3). He is loving (Luke 23:34) and glorious (John 13:31). He accepted worship and prayer and claimed to be the only way to God (John 14:6). He carries the same names as God: the rock (1 Cor. 10:4), stone (Luke 20:17), light (John 1:9), Savior (1 Tim. 4:10), redeemer (Isa. 59:20), Holy One (1 John 2:20), King (John 12:13), and first and last (Rev. 22:13).

(2) Romans 1:3—Paul said that God's message concerns His Son, "Jesus Christ our Lord, who was made of the seed of David according to the flesh, and declared to be the son of God with power, according to the spirit of holiness, by the resurrection from the dead." The writers of the New Testament always present Christ as both the son of David and the Son of God.

(3) 2 Timothy 2:8—Paul said, "Remember that Jesus Christ, of the seed of David, was raised from the dead according to my gospel." The seed of David refers to His humanness; His rising from the dead refers to His deity.

(4) Philippians 2:6-10—Christ, "being in the form of God, thought it not robbery to be equal with God, but made himself of no reputation, and took upon him the form of a servant, and was made in the likeness of men; and, being found in fashion as a man, he humbled himself and became obedient unto death, even the death of the cross. Wherefore, God also hath highly exalted him, and given him a name which is above every name, that at the name of Jesus every knee should bow."

(5) John 1:14—John said, "The word [Jesus] was made flesh, and dwelt among us (and we beheld his glory, the glory as of the only begotten of the Father), full of grace and truth." John and his contemporaries saw God as much as they saw man.

2. The determination

Theologian Bernard Ramm's classic approach to explaining the union of Christ's deity and humanity in his *Protestant Christian Evidences* deserves noting ([Chicago: Moody, 1953], pp. 166-83):

"If God became a man we would expect His human life to be sinless." Jesus was.

"If God were to become a man we would expect Him to be holy." Jesus was.

"If God were a man we would expect His words to be the greatest words ever spoken." Jesus' words were.

"If God were a man we would expect Him to exert a profound power over human personality." Jesus did.

"If God were a man we would expect supernatural doings." Jesus did them.

"If God were to become a man we would expect Him to manifest the love of God." And Jesus did that by dying on the cross.

IV. THE INAPPROPRIATE RESPONSE (v. 46)

"No man was able to answer him a word, neither dared any man from that day forth ask him any more questions."

A. Of the Crowd

Mark adds after this that the common people heard Jesus gladly (12:37). They wanted to hear more, but as followers they simply followed the trend of their leaders. In a few days, they were screaming for Jesus' blood (Matt. 27:20). Perhaps the multitude wanted to hear more from Him because they were still thinking He was the military hero they were looking for. When it became apparent that He would not overthrow the Roman government, they turned on Him.

B. Of the Pharisees

The Pharisees should have concluded that Jesus was both David's son and Lord. That was the only logical conclusion. If they had opened their hearts, they would have seen Him for what He was. However, they didn't. They asked Jesus carefully crafted questions and received profound answers—answers they did not expect. However, they rejected what He had to say, refusing to be embarrassed by whom they considered to be an upstart from Nazareth. Nevertheless they were hopelessly outclassed, and they knew it.

Conclusion

People today become so caught up in promoting their self-righteousness that they end up denying Christ and damning their souls. They become so wrapped up in themselves that they don't want to see or hear the truth. Countless believers have defended the deity of Christ with overwhelming evidence, yet people do not respond.

What is your response to the deity of Christ? All the evidence was presented, yet the Pharisees concluded He was a blasphemer (Matt. 26:65). Others silently walked away. A few may have believed. What is your response? Jesus Christ came into the world as a man to die for men and as God to gain the victory over death, sin, and hell. He truly is the perfect Savior.

The first person to whom Jesus revealed His identity was the Samaritan woman (John 4:5-29). She was looking for the Christ. He revealed to her that He was the Christ, and she was saved. It's a tragedy that today between 400 and 500 Samaritans on Mount Gerizim still wait for the Messiah. They don't believe He ever came the first time. What is your response?

Focusing on the Facts

1. What is the most important of all questions (see p. 76)?
2. What were some of the early opinions concerning Jesus Christ (see pp. 76-79)?
3. What is underneath many of the complementary descriptions of Jesus Christ (see p. 79)?
4. What is the doctrinal core of Christianity (see p. 79)?
5. Describe what at least three groups have said concerning the deity of Jesus Christ (see pp. 79-81).
6. True or false: Christ's deity is attacked more than any other Christian doctrine (see p. 79).
7. Of what did Jesus' twofold confrontation of the Pharisees consist (see p. 82)?
8. Why was Jesus indirect when asking the Pharisees a question about Himself (see p. 83)?
9. What was the standard Jewish reply to the question of whose son the Messiah was? Explain your answer using Scripture (see pp. 83-84).
10. Why does Matthew go into such great detail in describing the genealogy of Jesus Christ (see pp. 85-86)?
11. What can be deduced from the fact that the Pharisees never questioned the genealogy of Jesus (see p. 86)?
12. What is the significance of the term *kurios* when referring to Jesus (see p. 87)?
13. What qualifying phrase would force the Pharisees from thinking that David made a mistake in calling the Messiah "Lord"? What does this phrase mean (see p. 88)?
14. True or false: Psalm 110 is the psalm most frequently quoted in the New Testament (see p. 88).
15. What three things did Jesus want to communicate to the Pharisees about Psalm 110:1 (see p. 89)?
16. What is the meaning of the phrase "sit thou on my right hand, till I make thine enemies thy footstool" (Matt. 22:44; see p. 90)?
17. The heart of Christianity is that Jesus Christ is both _____ and _____ (see p. 92).
18. Describe the difference between the humanity and deity of Jesus Christ. Explain your answer from Scripture (see pp. 92-93).
19. What changed the minds of the common people who initially wanted to hear more from Jesus (see p. 94)?
20. To whom did Jesus first reveal His identity? What was that person's response (see p. 95)?

Pondering the Principles

1. There have been many opinions about Jesus Christ. Some hold Him as the supreme example of virtue, while others emphasize His love or wisdom. What is your opinion of Jesus Christ? Is He only a model for kind behavior toward others, or is He the God-man who came to take away the sin of the world? Your answer will determine your eternal destiny. Study the following passages and conclude from them your opinion of Jesus: John 1:1-18, Colossians 1:14-19, 1 Timothy 3:16, and Hebrews 1:1-3.

2. Through the centuries, many have struggled with the two great realities of Christ's nature—His humanity and His deity—and how they are fused into one Person. The following verses speak of both the humanity and deity of Christ: Philippians 2:6-10, Acts 17:31, and Hebrews 10:12. Study them. Take what you have learned and share it with someone you know is not a believer.

Scripture Index